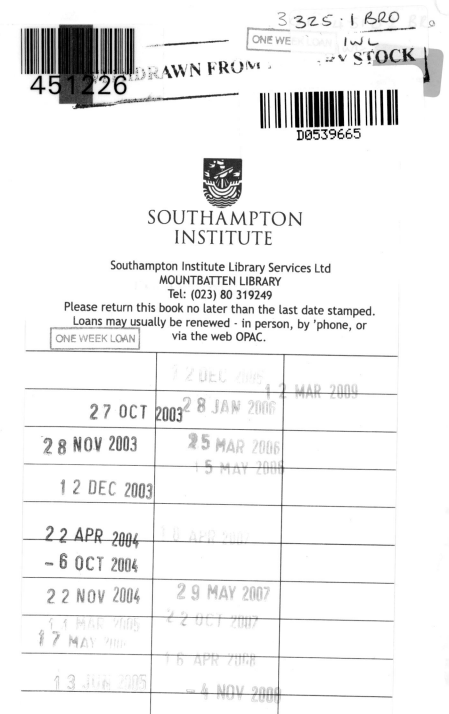

Do We Need Mass Immigration?

The economic, demographic, environmental, social and developmental arguments against large-scale net immigration to Britain

Anthony Browne

Civitas: Institute for the Study of Civil Society
London

First published November 2002

The Mezzanine, Elizabeth House
39 York Road, London SE1 7NQ
email: books@civitas.org.uk

ISBN 1-903 386-23-3

Typeset by Civitas
in New Century Schoolbook

Printed in Great Britain by
Hartington Fine Arts Ltd
Lancing, Sussex

Contents

Author

Anthony Browne is the Environment Editor of *The Times*. He has previously been Health Editor at the *Observer*, Deputy Business Editor at the *Observer*, Economics Correspondent at the *Observer*, and Economics Reporter at the BBC. He is also author of *The Euro—should Britain join?* (Icon Books).

Challenge to Critics

This book tries to raise serious issues about the future shape of our society and economy, how we adapt to population ageing and help global development in an informed and objective way, which I know will be met with much opposition. But simply making accusations of racism, pointing at the joys of diversity, or citing how many wonderful Vietnamese restaurants there are in London, avoids the debate. If substantive, coherent arguments are not raised in opposition to the points made, then one can only presume there are no such arguments.

The question that needs answering is:

Why would one of the world's most densely crowded islands, with a naturally growing population and a growing workforce, not suffering a demographic time bomb, with desperately overstretched public services, suffering from road congestion and overcrowded public transport, suffering from a housing crisis so severe that the government has to impose high density housing on communities who really don't want it, and which has a total of four million people out of work who want to work, including 1.5 million unemployed—why should such a country need immigration at such levels that it quadruples the rate of population growth, creates parallel societies and brings enough people to fill a city the size of Cambridge every six to eight months?

Why, also, should the rich world drain the Third World of its talent?

My answer is that Britain doesn't need—and as surveys repeatedly show, want—such levels of immigration. The answer is that the record net immigration that we are experiencing is not in the interests of the British or even generally in the interest of the countries from where the immigrants come, although it is in the interests of the immigrants themselves. What's your answer?

Executive Summary

This report is not anti-immigration or anti-immigrant, but argues that the current record wave of immigration is unsustainable and both detrimental to the interests of many people in Britain and against the wishes of the majority of people in Britain. It argues that Britain does not have a moral duty to accept immigration, and that immigration is ineffective as a global development policy. It argues for immigration that is balanced, with equal numbers of people coming and going, and that is in the interests of people in Britain rather than just in the interests of potential immigrants, recent immigrants and businesses that like cheap labour. The immigration system should command the acceptance and confidence of the people of Britain. It also argues that the government should pursue an open borders policy in so far as this is compatible with balanced and sustainable migration, such as negotiating an open border policy with Japan.

The UK is experiencing the highest levels of net immigration in its history, quadrupling the rate of population growth and adding 543,000 to the population in the last three years, and 1.02m to the population between 1992 and 2000.

The level of net legal immigration has grown from 35,000 in 1993 to 183,000 in 2000 (the difference between 482,000 arriving and 299,000 leaving). On top of this is an unknown amount of illegal immigration.

Unless immigration declines, it will add more than two million people every ten years. The Government Actuary Service estimates that with immigration of 195,000 a year (very close to the present level of legal immigration), the UK population will grow from 59.8m in 2000 to 68.0m in 2031. On present trends, around 6m of the 8m increase in population will move to London and the South East.

This is a completely different phenomenon from earlier waves of immigration, such as Huguenots, Jews and Ugandan Asians, all of whom were forced to leave their country of origin, and were limited in number and so the immigration had a natural conclusion.

The present record level of immigration is because Britain is rich, much of the world is poor, and there are many routes for people in the poor parts of the world to get here to improve their lives. For the first time in human history, we have simultaneously huge disparities of wealth across the world; extensive knowledge in the poor parts about how the rich world lives and how to get there, through television, mass media and cheap global telecommunications; and cheap rapid transport across the globe.

This immigration pressure is reflected in the fact that every single category of immigration has grown, including family reunion (people bringing in husbands, wives, children, parents and grandparents), asylum, work permits, and students who settle permanently.

Whatever the route of entry, it is ultimately economically driven because all the record net immigration is from low-income countries to the UK; between the UK and the rest of the developed world, there is roughly balanced migration, with equal numbers of people coming and going.

This record net immigration is presumably good for the immigrants, otherwise they would not come, or having come, would go home. However it is not in the interests of the majority of the people of Britain, nor is it particularly good for the countries they come from.

However, the imperative to combat racism has resulted in a concerted campaign to convince the people of Britain that immigration in such record numbers is in their own interest. This has created a number of widely believed immigration myths that are simply untrue:

- Britain does not have a declining population—more babies are born each year than people die, and this is expected to carry on for another twenty years. The Government Actuary Service predicts that, with zero net migration, the population will grow very gently from 59.8m in 2000 to 60.3 in 2020.

- Britain does not have a declining workforce, but the fastest growing workforce in Europe. This is largely due to the increase in retirement age of women from 60 to 65 between 2010 and 2020. The Government Actuary Service predicts that, with zero net immigration, the workforce will grow by 1.2m by 2020, from 36.89m in 2000 to 38.127 in 2020.
- Britain is not suffering a demographic time bomb, with an unsupportable burden of pensioners on the working population. Rather, the ratio of economically dependent children and pensioners compared to the working-age population is expected to get more benign over the next 20 years. The Government Actuary Service predicts that the number of children and pensioners per thousand people of working age will fall from 620 in 2000 to 583 in 2020.
- Britain is not suffering from generalised labour shortages —according to the Labour Force Survey there are 1.55 million unemployed in the UK, with an extra 2.3m who are out of work and want to work but don't look largely because they don't think they will be able to get jobs that pay well enough. We are also part of a single labour market, the EU, which has 13.4m unemployed, a number which is set to be increased sharply when Eastern Europe is given free movement of people in the EU in the next ten years or so.
- As recognised by every authority and study on the issue (including the Government Actuary Service, the Home Office, the Council of Europe and OECD), immigration is no 'fix' for an ageing population, because immigrants grow old too. An ageing society is utterly inevitable, and Britain will have to create policies to adjust to it, irrespective of whether there is immigration or not.
- Immigration does boost GDP, but there is no evidence that it raises the level of the one measure that matters, GDP per capita, and unskilled immigration that leads to immigrant communities with high unemployment rates

and low incomes may actually lower it. Nor does immigration raise the long-term economic growth rate, and may actually lower it because, by increasing the population, it increases the economically constraining effects of land shortages and congestion. Despite its dependence on immigration, GDP per capita in the US has grown no faster than Europe.

- Immigrants overall do pay more in tax than they receive in benefits and consume in public services, but only because immigrants from North America, Japan and the EU pay so much more than their fair share. Immigrants from the Third World—who make up the entire net immigration to the UK—are on average less well educated, suffer higher unemployment, claim more of most forms of benefits, make more demands on public services such as schools and hospitals, and almost certainly do not pay their way on average. There are no figures for the UK, but official studies in the US show that the average adult Mexican immigrant will consume throughout their life time $55,200 more in services than they contribute in taxes. The studies show that each immigrant without high school education consumes $89,000 more in benefits and services than they pay in taxes. Households in California, where most Mexican immigrants arrive, have to pay on average $1,178 more in taxes each year to subsidise them.
- Immigration is culturally enriching, although there are decreasing economies of scale to this in that doubling the amount of immigration doesn't double the amount of cultural enrichment. There is also little evidence that British people actually want to be culturally enriched by immigration from around the globe, any more than the people of Nigeria, India, Saudi Arabia or China do.

The scale and type of immigration currently being experienced in the UK can also be damaging to the interests of many groups of people in the UK, although there are winners and losers:

- Those who benefit from immigration are those who employ immigrants—such as companies who like plentiful cheap labour and people who like cheap cleaners; those who lose from immigration are those who compete with immigrants, most notably unskilled workers and those from British ethnic minorities. The US government estimates that about half the decline in wages of unskilled workers in US is because of competition from unskilled immigrants.
- The immigration-led rapid growth in population sharply increases the demand for new houses and, if it carries on at current rates, will increase demand for homes by two million by 2021, pushing up the pressure to build on green belt land, pushing up house prices, adding to congestion, overcrowding in the South East and pollution.
- Immigration as currently configured increases inequalities in the UK because it causes a massive redistribution of wealth from those who compete with immigrants in the labour market (who tend to be poor, and suffer lower wages), to those who employ them (who tend to be rich, and enjoy lower costs and bigger profits). This effect is well documented in the US. In addition, in the UK, with its tight property market, those who win are those who already own property, particularly those who rent it out; and those who lose are those who rent their homes and those trying to get on the property ladder. Again, this is generally a redistribution of wealth from poor to rich.
- Immigration makes the UK a more unbalanced country because around three-quarters of immigrants move to the South East and London. This is likely to be partially offset by less internal migration from the north of England to London, because of the higher London property prices and increasing overcrowding which discourages internal migration to London, and encourages internal emigration from London to elsewhere in the UK.
- Large-scale immigration without integration causes social fragmentation. This is increasingly seen in northern towns such as Bradford, where official studies

suggest that segregation and alienation between communities is getting worse. Immigration at a slower rate gives more time for integration.

- Immigration is not a substitute for a development policy. It deprives many poor countries of their most educated and entrepreneurial citizens, often devastating health and education systems essential to development, and depriving developing countries of tax-paying and politically stabilising middle-classes. One third of educated Ghanains and Sierra Leoneons, and 75 per cent of educated Jamaicans, live abroad. This is mitigated by remittances, but dependence on remittances encourages developing countries to become remittance economies based on exporting their educated members and does nothing to stimulate their economies in ways that make people want to live there rather than leave.

However, immigration clearly benefits immigrants. Any immigration policy must balance the cost and benefits of immigration on those groups of UK residents who win, those who lose, and the benefits to immigrants, would-be immigrants and the source countries. The current UK immigration policy is geared primarily to the interests of immigrants and big business which likes cheap labour, with little consideration of its wider impact on British residents, environment or economy.

The current levels of immigration, which create parallel societies and are resented by the majority of British people, fuel racial tensions. If an immigration system is seen by the British people to be genuinely in their interests, and commands their confidence, then they are likely to be far more welcoming to those that come.

A rational immigration policy must explicitly identify its aim, the ways to achieve that aim, and then it must be enforced. It must be rational enough to withstand open debate, and attract widespread public support. The immigration policy should balance the humanitarian (asylum and family reunion), with some limited economic ends such as filling specific skills shortages.

To achieve these ends it must identify both the optimal scale of net immigration, and the optimal types of immigrants. Since Britain is one of the world's most crowded countries, with a naturally growing population, the optimal level of net migration is zero or mildly negative.

Zero net migration does not mean 'fortress Britain'—it means equal numbers coming and going. Those coming will include a proportion of refugees, as well as children, husbands and wives. It should also include a proportion that are highly skilled, particularly those with skills that are in short supply in the UK—such as heart surgeons.

Immigration, in allowing people to move to where they can maximise their welfare and get maximum return on their skills, is a definite force for good in the world, so long as it doesn't lead to unbalanced, unsustainable and destabilising population flows. Therefore, the UK government should aim at policies that allow as free a movement of people as is compatible with having balanced and sustainable migration, as has been achieved within the EU. Britain should initiate negotiations on having an open border policy with other high-income countries such as Japan, where migration flows are likely to be limited, balanced and beneficial.

Personal Introduction and Apologia

It may come as a surprise that someone writing a book that is apparently anti-immigration is himself the son of an immigrant, living with an immigrant, who is from such a family of émigrés that he has virtually no relatives in the country where he lives, with every single aunt, uncle, grandparent, and first cousin living overseas in four different countries, and known extended family in a dozen countries including Denmark, Norway, Italy, France, Ireland, the USA, South Africa, Australia and Zimbabwe.

The reasons for my family's movements span the spectrum of motivations: my grandmother emigrated from the UK to Kenya after the war for health reasons after my grandfather was killed by the Nazis; my mother immigrated to the UK for love and to escape the parochialism and hardship of post-Nazi-occupied Norway; my partner's parents emigrated from Ireland to Canada to take up a specific job, and she emigrated from Canada to the UK to pursue education and stayed on for love (she tells me).

Moreover, I believe that immigration, in getting cultures to mix and learn from each other, in letting people better their lives in a country of their choice and helping them escape persecution, can be an enormously powerful and positive force for good. Immigration has undoubtedly enriched Britain over the centuries, just as it has built America, Australia and Canada into the countries they are. But immigration policies should be sustainable, shown to balance the interests of immigrants and native population, and have the approval of the population already there.

I am certainly not anti-immigration, certainly not anti-immigrant, or somehow xenophobic about foreigners or driven by a deep racism. After all, virtually my entire family are foreigners, and they are not all white. I myself have had three long-term relationships with women of colour, all children of immigrants to the UK.

But my background also gives me a certain comfortableness about the concept and issues surrounding immigration, the process, the consequences, the rights, the duties, a comfortableness which so many people in Britain clearly lack (as it happens, many of the most high-profile advocates of curbing immigration to the US, such as Peter Brimelow, George Borjas, and Yeh Ling-Ling are themselves immigrants to that country).

Indeed, it is not going too far to say that Britain as a country has a major neurosis about immigration. And that national neurosis means that the public debate is more an expression of national psychological hang-ups than an expression of rational thought, and ensures the national debate about immigration is about as ill-informed and hypocritical as the Victorian discourse was about sex. Many people are extremely uncomfortable about saying in front of strangers anything other than the official line that all immigration is good, whoever the immigrants are and whatever their numbers.

If a modern person without particular hang ups about sex, its power, its joy, its misery, lived in Victorian England, they would probably feel like screaming out about it and say: chill out and think honestly. That's how I feel about the British public discourse on immigration.

My training as a mathematician gives me too much respect for truth to suppress it to political convenience. My career as a journalist gives me too much respect for freedom of speech to let fear of the inevitable accusations of racism make me silent. History shows that silence only serves the devil. Modern liberal democracies were built on debate.

Immigration is one of the world's most powerful forces, often for good, but not always. It is also an incredibly complex phenomenon, undertaken for countless reasons, by countless peoples, from countless backgrounds, going to countless destinations, with countless consequences.

The so-called First Nation Americans felt that the flood of European immigration was not good for them, even if it was good for the Europeans themselves. Slaves forced to emigrate from modern day Ghana to the American South would have thought it wasn't good for them, even if it was good for the whites already there. Immigration helped build the US into the most powerful nation on earth, taking tens of millions out of poverty and away from intolerance. Native Canary Islanders complain about the invasion of the English, protesting: '*las Canarias por los Canarios*.'

The ridiculous naivety of our national debate about immigration is shown by the fact that almost everyone can describe themselves as either for or against immigration. Taking such a position is about as sensible as saying you are for or against sex: only someone of a Victorian mindset could say such a thing. Think about it a bit and most people would conclude they are against rape, against incest, either for or against one-night-stands with strangers, and for sex within a loving committed relationship.

The debates about immigration in such thoroughly immigrant nations as Canada, America and Australia are far deeper, complex and somewhat more honest than our own. People take stances, and have points to prove, but realise the many-faceted nature of immigration. Government studies can point to both costs and benefits of immigration to different groups within society, and campaign groups set up to change some but not all immigration policies. Politics dictates that official studies in Britain have to conclude that all immigration is good in every way, a free lunch for the British people. It isn't.

Both Canada and Australia see no contradiction between having active immigration programmes from countries across the world, while reacting strongly against boat-loads of people, many of whom have paid people-traffickers, turning up on their shores. They want immigration, but want to set the terms of it. Few in Britain are capable of making such a fundamental distinction: we basically have no active immigration policy, but just let those who turn up stay.

My biggest concern in writing this is not of knee-jerk accusations of racism, which so often come from those who make their living and reputation out of pointing fingers at others. I am certainly concerned that racist bigots will see this as a justification of their hatred, but extremists should not be allowed to silence the debate. As the continued low level of support for the BNP shows, the vast majority of people in Britain are not extremists, and are generally tolerant.

But my biggest concern is that many members of ethnic minorities who I like and respect and who are as British as me—if not more so—will take offence at what I write. If you do, sincerest, deepest apologies: please don't read into this book motives and thoughts that are not there.

Preface

The Human Rights Principles that Underlie this Work

I assume in this book certain human rights principles, which I believe should be inalienable and should not be compromised for political expediency.

- Everyone has the right not to be subjected to discrimination of any sort, including racial discrimination.
- Everyone has the right to be accepted as a full and equal citizen in the country they were born and grew up in. Ethnic minorities born in the UK are as British as a white person whose family has been here for centuries. It is deeply unjust that in certain Middle East states, and formerly in Germany, immigrant workers' children who are born in the country and have lived in it all their lives are denied citizenship. White Zimbabweans who were born there, and indeed whose families emigrated there generations ago, have a right to be considered full Zimbabweans.
- Every nation has the right to decide who can move there and who can't. States have a fundamental right to protect the integrity of their borders.
- Everyone with a genuine fear of persecution by their government should have the right to asylum.

1

The dishonesty of the immigration debate

It is the biggest debate of our age, and yet a non-debate: officially everyone agrees. The *Financial Times* declares that 'Europe needs immigrants—skilled and unskilled'. *Time Magazine* informs its readers that large-scale immigration to Europe is 'inevitable', that Europe cannot survive without it. All mainstream political parties agree we need immigration, even if they bicker over ways to maintain the integrity of the asylum laws.

This startling consensus about a subject as complex and far-reaching as immigration, about which the public clearly feel massive unease, reflects the success of a sustained campaign by pro-immigrationists to deny any counter arguments, shame anyone who suggests possible downsides of immigration by accusing them of scaremongering and racism, and to promote arguments for immigration, whether based on fact or not.

The repeated trumpeting of arguments for immigration without any critical examination has resulted in many often repeated and widely believed immigration myths—for example, that Britain has a declining population or dwindling workforce, when both are actually growing and the government expects them to carry on growing for the next 20 years. All the arguments given to justify immigration are in fact post-facto justifications of immigration that has already happened, and most of which happened for the simple reason that immigrants wanted to come to the UK to improve their lives and because employers like cheap labour.

The determination of the pro-immigrationists reflects the fact that immigration as an issue has become a substitute for race; the imperative to combat racism has transmuted into the imperative to promote immigration.

This febrile atmosphere means that when the UK's top labour economist wrote to a national newspaper pointing out that unskilled people lose out from competition with unskilled immigrants, he was rewarded with letters accusing him of racism. It means that housing forecasters play down the impact of immigration on housing demand. It means that demographers have feared losing their jobs if they were to do 'ethnic mix projections' forecasting the make-up of British society if current trends continue (something that the US government does).

There are also huge, co-ordinated and often taxpayer-funded vested interests in promoting immigration, whereas the opposition is widespread and unfocussed. Many, such as environment groups, trade unions and mainstream politicians, are easily silenced by fear of appearing racist. The promotion of immigration in the UK has become an unholy alliance between big business, which likes cheap labour; ethnic lobbies, which want to increase the size of their communities; universities, who want to bring over fee-paying students; anti-race campaigners who fear the rise of the British National Party; and the immigration industry, including advisers, lawyers and people traffickers, who profit out of immigration and so want more of it.

The result is that immigration is more characterised by distortion, denial and hostility to debate than any other public issue. Such a distorted, one-sided debate would be inconceivable in any other area of such national importance, whether economics, law and order, or defence.

As public concern about immigration has grown, so the pro-immigrationists imperative to promote more immigration has meant that all counter arguments have had to be neutralised, even if that means a complete U-turn on previously held positions. In the late 1990s, governments of all major industrialised nations signed passionate communiqués about how mass unemployment was the biggest problem facing modern society. Then immigration reared its head, and suddenly it is mass labour shortages that are the biggest problem of our time. From labour surplus to labour shortage in a few short years—how intellectual fashions flutter in the political wind!

Unskilled young men, predominantly black, were being alienated and facing a bleak future because of the shortage of unskilled jobs for them—until immigration reared its head. Now there are suddenly far too many unskilled and so we have to have unskilled immigrants.

History is rewritten to fit the thesis that everyone mu support. When Japan's economy collapsed, it was becaus Japan had an asset bubble that burst after decades of record growth and an institutional inability to reform the banking system, but since then immigration has reared its head, and we suddenly discover that Japan is in recession because it doesn't accept immigrants (although lack of immigrants didn't stop Japan becoming one of the richest nations on earth, and the world's second largest economy, or Norway becoming one of the richest countries on earth with a higher quality of life than any other country, according to the UNDP).

Instead of being a nation with ancient traditions where the vast majority can trace their families back to the time of William the Conquerer, Britain suddenly becomes a nation of immigrants like America.

On the other hand, ask why Britain, one of the most densely populated countries in the world, should want a growing population and you are unlikely to get an answer. No one dares question whether immigrant groups suffering unemployment rates of over 50 per cent are really that effective a way of meeting any labour shortages. No one dares mention the obvious point that if we import large numbers of poor and unskilled people into a highly skilled economy it is likely to add to poverty rather than help eradicate it. It took a remarkably long time for the media and politicians to take on board the simple point that people who go from France, where they are not being persecuted, to the UK must have some motives other than fleeing persecution that they may have faced on the other side of the world, several countries ago.

The debate about immigration is the most dishonest one in Britain at the start of the twentieth century: it is not about truth, but about politics, and particularly the politics of race.

So when, in this political climate, the Home Office writes a report on whether or not immigrants are subsidised by native taxpayers, there could politically only be one answer.

It would be impossible for the Home Office to say anything other than that immigrants are net contributors to the public coffers (in the US, Sweden and other countries, there is much evidence that the exact opposite is true.)

It leads to incredibly biased media coverage. The Dutch politician Pim Fortuyn was hysterically denounced for being racist, even though he had many black supporters and his deputy was black; only after he was assassinated did the shock force the media to admit that his ideas were far more balanced and complex, and that they had gone too far turning him into a bogeyman. The affair made Dutch people aware of just how much anti-racist witch-hunting can itself engender hate, with newspapers concluding that those who demonised Fortuyn 'may not have pulled the trigger, but they pointed the gun.'

Immigration is one of the most important issues facing Britain, and we owe it to all the people of Britain, present residents and future generations, to be honest about it. And there is an honest debate to be had, recognising there are benefits as well as drawbacks. The pro-immigration lobby must challenge itself to accept there are drawbacks, such as growing crowding and congestion, and that while some parts of society may gain, others may lose, and that all people have the right to oppose changes to their society imposed from outside. Simply responding to a book like this with accusations of racism, or trumpeting the odd (but hopefully not inevitable!) factual error, rather than responding to the general arguments, is a cheap and disingenuous way to repeat the pattern of avoiding real debate.

Similarly, those who are against immigration must accept there are some benefits to the economy of some forms of immigration, particularly for employers, and that many people do actually like increased cultural diversity.

We are sliding into an unprecedented programme of using large-scale immigration as a tool of economic and demographic policy that will utterly transform British society, and yet we cannot honestly debate the merits and demerits of it. The historical scale of what we are embarking on is only matched by the folly of not clearly thinking it through.

Why opposing large-scale immigration is not racist

It seems likely that the ultimate motivation for many people who are opposed to immigration is essentially racism, just as the ultimate motivation for many people who promote immigration is a dislike of Britain and things British, and a desire to change society. It is also true that the only political party standing on the anti-immigration platform is the avowedly racist British National Party.

But race and immigration are separate if overlapping issues, and the equating of the two masks the fact that you can quite validly have different opinions on each. Many people in Britain who certainly do not consider themselves racist, are very concerned about the sheer scale that immigration has now reached and about the failure of significant minorities to integrate.

It also means that immigration is generally just seen as immigration of non-whites, whereas obviously whites over the last few centuries have been the great migrant race. Even now, a large component of immigration to the UK is white people, from the EU, from East Europe, Oceania and North America.

Many ethnic minorities—and even ethnic immigrants—are opposed to further immigration. A survey by the Commission for Racial Equality showed that 46 per cent of ethnic minorities think there is too much immigration to the UK. The former deputy leader of the Dutch anti-immigration party Fortuyn's List was a black immigrant from Cape Verde. Winston Peters, the former deputy prime minister of New Zealand and the leader of the explicitly immigration-restrictionist party New Zealand First, is half-Maori and half-Scottish.

In the US, there is an anti-immigration group made up explicitly of ethnic minorities, called the Diversity Alliance, founded by an immigrant from Vietnam who worked in the immigration industry before concluding it was getting out of hand. They conducted an opinion poll which showed that 65 per cent of black Americans favour a moratorium on legal immigration. One of the leading immigration reform journalists in the US is Michelle Malkin, an Asian-American, and author of *Invasion*. Many of the founders of the black rights movement in the US were anti-immigrant, because of the effect immigration was having in undermining African-Americans in the labour market (see below p. 7).

There are many other motives to oppose immigration, which are honourable and nothing to do with racism. Samuel Gompers, the founder of the American Federation of Labor, was a Jewish immigrant who supported the early twentieth-century immigration cut-off in the US. In a 1924 letter to Congress, Gompers wrote:

> Every effort to enact immigration legislation must expect to meet a number of hostile forces and, in particular, two hostile forces of considerable strength. One of these is composed of corporation employers who desire to employ physical strength at the lowest possible wage and who prefer a rapidly revolving labor supply at low wages to a regular supply of American wage-earners at fair wages. The other is composed of racial groups in the United States who oppose all restrictive legislation because they want the doors left open for an influx of their countrymen.

Only in the last few years has the AFL stopped its opposition to immigration, because it wants to recruit more Hispanic immigrants as members. The American Engineering Association remains an immigration-reformer in order to protect its members' interests.

Most of the founders of the main environment groups in North America are anti-immigrant because of the impact immigration has on fuelling population growth and so on the environment. The US's leading environment group, the Sierra Club, was for a long time anti-immigration, but dropped its opposition recently because its liberal members were concerned about appearing racist.

Paul Watson, one of the founders of Greenpeace, and the founder of the Sea Shepherd Conservation Society, has said:

> The accusation that a stand to reduce immigration is racist is music to the ears to those who profit from the cheap labor of immigrants. They are the same people who love to see environmen-

talists make fools of themselves. And there is no environmentalist more foolish than one who refuses to confront the fact that uncontrolled human population growth is the No. 1 cause of the world's increasing environmental problems.

Critics of those who oppose large-scale immigration make the implicit assumption that if you are anti-immigration you must be anti-immigrant, or an immigrant-basher. However, saying someone who is opposed to large-scale immigration is anti-immigrant is like saying that someone who is in favour of family planning is anti-baby, or that someone who thinks that the world's population has grown too large simply hates people. As I mentioned in my personal introduction, many of the leading critics of large-scale immigration in the USA are themselves immigrants, and many of the leading US immigration reform groups are at pains to say 'no to immigrant-bashing' and 'immigrants welcome here'.

The confusion between being anti-immigration and anti-immigrant is politically convenient for those who wish to push for more immigration, but it runs the risk of promoting racism. (See chapter 29.)

****

African-Americans and Immigration

When Frederick Douglass escaped slavery in the American south in the 1830s and headed north, he saw the beginnings of immigrant competition with blacks. Black men and women at the time earned relatively good wages as labourers, house servants, porters, butlers, maids, cooks, laundresses and seamstresses. But the influx of white foreigners meant that unskilled European workers moved into these occupations prepared to take lower wages, reducing blacks' earnings dramatically and depriving many of employment.

In an 1853 article, Douglass commented: 'The old avocations, by which colored men obtained a livelihood, are rapidly, unceasingly and inevitably passing into other hands; every hour sees the black man elbowed out of employment by some newly arrived emigrant. It is evident, pain-

fully evident to every reflecting mind, that the means of living, for colored men, are becoming more and more precarious and limited. Employments and callings, formerly monopolized by us, are so no longer.'

In an 1879 article in the Baltimore Sun, he observed how the bargaining power of blacks, potentially greater in the South because of a lack of other labour, was undercut in the immigrant-rich cities of the North: 'Our people in the South have a monopoly of the labor market. They are the arm, the muscle and the hand, with the vantage ground of the constitution behind them, men sympathizing with them in every State, and the power to say, "Give us fair wages or your fields will go untilled." In the North and West they will have no such advantage.'

In a 1904 article, 'Bread and Butter Argument', The Colored American Magazine *described the displacement of blacks by immigrants: 'In a broader way the statistics just furnished by the Federal Census Bureau show that there has been a steady falling off in the number of Negroes employed in the skilled trades. White artisans, of their own motion or by motion of the trades union, are crowding them hard if not out.'*

Many leading black rights campaigners were opposed to immigration. Philip Randolph, who obtained the nation's first fair employment policy by threatening a march on Washington, said in 1924: 'Instead of reducing immigration to two percent of the 1890 quota, we favour reducing it to nothing... We favour shutting out the Germans from Germany, the Italians from Italy...the Hindus from India, the Chinese from China, and even the Negroes from the West Indies. This country is suffering from immigrant indigestion.'

The decline of immigration during and after World War I showed how much black life could improve when there were fewer foreigners in the North, with shortages of labour allowing them to move from the cotton fields to the factories.

In 1928, the Courier *newspaper summed up the benefits for black Americans of ending mass immigration: 'So far as the Negro is concerned, it is exceedingly doubtful whether he has been benefited by these successive waves of foreign labor. Indeed, there is good reason to believe that the economic progress of our group has been hindered by immigration. As proof, one has only to point to the great strides made by Negroes, in all classes, since European immigration has been so markedly curtailed. This is especially noticeable in the North and East, where, despite the present temporary period of unemployment, the Negro has more industrial opportunities than at any time since the Civil War.'*

The leading black newspaper, the Chicago Defender, *insisted in 1924 that immigration should continue to be kept at low levels: 'It is vitally important to keep the immigration gates partly closed until our working class gets a chance to prove our worth in occupations other than those found on plantations. The scarcity of labour creates the demand. With the average American white man's turn of mind, the white foreign labourer is given preference over the black home product. When the former is not available, the latter gets an inning.'*

Frank L. Morris, former dean of graduate studies at Morgan State University in Baltimore, warned in a foreword for the Centre for Immigration Studies pamphlet Cast Down Your Bucket Where You Are *that the same was happening again, and blamed the current malaise of many blacks on immigration. 'The mass immigration that started in the late 19th century greatly slowed the industrialization of the South and has made Southern rural poverty most difficult to eradicate. We are beginning to reap the policy whirlwind of a similar mass immigration policy in the 1980s and 1990s. The result has been similar—a more difficult and depressed labour market for African-Americans in the last part of the 20th century. African-Americans are disproportionately hurt by this process because immigrants tend to locate in our big cities, there to compete with African-Americans for housing, jobs, and education. Anything, including immigration, which increases the supply of labour in America works against the interests of African-Americans.'*

3

Why zero net immigration is not Fortress Britain

Those who argue against immigration are often accused of having a Fortress Britain, or a Fortress Europe, mentality. They are accused of wanting to put up razor-wire barricades around the borders, shutting off Britain and Europe from the rest of the world. Some do want that and are indeed xenophobes with whom I would have little in common. Immigration, the freedom of people to move to pursue better lives and escape persecution, has historically been a force for good, bringing new ideas and revitalising societies, and it remains a force for good now.

But wanting balanced immigration, or zero net immigration, is not the same as wanting Fortress Britain. Indeed, wanting balanced immigration is totally compatible with having a generally open immigration policy, with open borders allowing people to come and go, so long as there are no forces in place to unleash huge flows of population one way or another.

As table 1 (p. 11) shows, large numbers of people both migrated to and emigrated from Britain in 2000, but net immigration was a record high of 183,000 because of a large imbalance between immigrants and emigrants: while 482,000 people arrived, only 299,000 people left. As the table shows, this imbalance is totally due to the imbalance of immigration to and from developing nations.

Wanting balanced or zero net immigration doesn't mean that you don't want anyone to come or go, merely that the numbers should be roughly equal. Indeed, under the right circumstances, balanced migration is compatible with extremely high levels of immigration and emigration. In fact, the region that the UK has the most balanced migration with is the region that it has the most open borders with and exchanges the most people with: the European Union.

Table 1
Origins and Destinations of Immigration To and From the UK in 2000 (thousands)

	Total	EU	Australia New Zealand Canada	USA	South Africa	India Bangladesh Sri Lanka	Pakistan	Caribbean	Other Common-wealth countries (mainly in Africa)	Middle East	Other foreign countries	High income	Low income
In	482	96	66	25	23	35	15	6	49	28	139	187	295
Out	299	99	73	34	9	3	2	2	14	13	49	206	92
Net	183	-3	-8	-9	15	32	13	4	35	14	91	-19	203

Source: Office for National Statistics
Note: figures do not add up due to rounding

The UK gets far more immigrants from the EU than it does from India, Bangladesh, Sri Lanka, Pakistan, the Caribbean and the Middle East combined. But the difference is that it is balanced: roughly the same number left Britain to move to Europe. With India, Bangladesh, Sri Lanka, Pakistan, the Caribbean, the Middle East and Africa, the immigration is almost totally one sided.

A large component of the emigration figure to the EU will be returners—French and Spanish youngsters who come to work in London for a few years, and then counted as emigrants on the way back. Some of it will be permanent or at least semi-permanent, such as German and Italian bankers pursuing their career in Britain, or British people retiring to the south of France and Spain. This is immigration at its best—allowing people to pursue their lives where they think is best, working in a balanced and sustainable way. Apart from some grumbles from the native inhabitants in Provence and the Canary Islands about being swamped by British people, the open border policy of the EU is generally seen as a huge success.

Despite the tighter immigration controls with Australasia and North America, there is roughly the same pattern of relatively balanced and sustainable migration. There is some net emigration, but the scale is small compared to the total flow of people. While a total of 91,000 people arrived from those two regions, 107,000 left. The net emigration from Britain to North America, Australasia and the EU is 19,000, or only about ten per cent of the total flow of people to the UK from those regions.

While migration with high-income countries is roughly balanced and sustainable, it is not with low-income countries. The figures from the Office of National Statistics do not give a detailed enough breakdown to classify Japan and South Korea as part of the rich world (although I would expect the figures to be small), but if you aggregate them into the figures for all the developing world, the pattern of huge imbalanced migration is stark.

While 295,000 arrived, 92,000 left, a ratio of more than three to one, resulting in a net immigration from the developing world of 203,000. This imbalance is obviously just a reflection of the imbalance of incomes between Britain and the rest of the world. These figures and arguments should illustrate that wanting policies that roughly result in zero net immigration—policies that promote balanced migration to and from Britain—does not mean pursuing Fortress Britain or Fortress Europe, but potentially quite the opposite.

4

Britain does not have a declining population

Given the common perception that Britain needs immigration to counter its dwindling population, it may come as a bit of a surprise to learn that actually Britain does not have a dwindling population, but a growing one. There are more births each year than deaths—in 1999, there were 700,000 births and 629,000 deaths, a natural population increase of 71,000 new people even before any immigration.

Nor is our population about to start dwindling any time in the near future. Britain actually has higher fertility rates than most other European countries, and it has one of the fastest naturally growing populations. Despite declining fertility, the pattern of having more births than deaths is expected to continue for at least twenty years. The population is then expected to start declining gradually, but such long-range projections are widely regarded as unreliable and should not form the basis of current policy.

Table 2
UK Population Projection (millions)

Year	2000	2010	2020	2031
Population with zero net immigration	59.8	60.1	60.3	59.6
Population with immigration of 195,000/year	59.8	62.4	65.3	68.0

Source: Government Actuary Service, 2000-based population projection, high migration and natural change only variants

The UK Government Actuary Service predicts that with zero net immigration, the population of Britain would rise very gently from 59.8m in 2000 to 60.3m in 2020, before gently declining back to the 2000 level by 2031.

In contrast, its high migration variant, which assumes immigration of 195,000, shows what will happen if the UK continues to attract levels of immigration as high as they have been in the last few years (legal immigration has been averaging about 180,000 and on top of that there is an unknown amount of illegal immigration). The population will rise from 59.8m to 68m by 2031, and then rises to over 70m. In other words, immigration at current levels will add about 10 million to the UK population.

The government assumes that immigration will decline of its own accord to 135,000 per year, in which case the population grows to 64.8m by 2025, and then peaks at 66m by 2040.

In its report *Replacement Migration*, which the pro-immigration lobby cite as supporting the need for immigration to combat a declining population, the United Nations actually predicted that even if the UK had no immigration at all, its population would still be larger in 2030 than in 1995.

The population of Europe is also expected to carry on growing. Eurostat, the EU's statistical agency, predicts that the population of the EU will grow from 376m in 2000 to 386m in 2025, an average annual growth rate of 0.1 per cent.

Although in the short term—up to 20 years—demographic projections are reasonably accurate, beyond that they have to be treated with caution. The long-range forecasts are based on assumptions about the fertility of women who haven't even been born yet, and yet fertility goes up as well as down, responding to changes in lifestyles and policies such as childcare provision.

It is not rational to base current policy on unreliable long-term forecasts. What we can be sure of is that the population is naturally increasing now, is highly likely to carry on doing so for about twenty years, and beyond that it is largely guesswork.

If the population does start declining in several decades, and we decide we don't like it, we can quickly turn on the immigration tap at that point. But hypothetical population decline is no justification to encourage large-scale immigration at the present time.

5

Britain does not have a declining workforce

Even if Britain's population isn't dwindling, it is often said that its workforce is. Actually, Britain's workforce is not declining, nor is it expected to for the next 20 years.

In fact, largely because of raising the level of women's retirement age from 60 to 65 between 2010 and 2020, the Government Actuary Service predicts that the workforce will expand by about 1.2m people in the next 20 years. It will then decline slightly, but even by 2031 the workforce will be the same size as it is now.

Table 3
UK Workforce with Zero Net Immigration (millions)

Year	2000	2010	2020	2031
Workforce (millions of people of working age)	36.89	37.39	38.13	36.82
Workforce as % of total population	61.7%	62.2%	63.2%	61.2%

Source: Government Actuary Service, 2000-based projections, natural change only variant

Furthermore, the number of actual workers—as opposed to people of working age—is expected to rise because of rising participation. That is, more of those of working age are actually expected to be available for work, because of the increased entry of women into the labour market, and the decline in early retirement.

The Council of Europe's 2001 study *Europe's Population and Labour Market Beyond 2000* predicted that the UK's active labour force would rise from 28.0m in 1999 to 29.8m in 2011, with 1.3m of the rise because of a continuing increase in the participation of women in the workforce and the trend of increasing part-time working among students.

Surveying a similar situation across Europe, it concluded that almost all the immigrant labour is the result of 'push migration' increasing the supply of it, rather than because immigrant labour is actually needed:

> Demand for immigrant labour is likely to be low. High unemployment levels and continuing increases in productivity make it very unlikely that a general labour shortage will appear in Europe. On the supply side, however, strong pressures will probably persist.

The *European Journal of Population* contained an extended evaluation of the widely-held belief that Europe needed immigration because it was facing a declining working population, and concluded that it was false. The study, 'Active Population Growth and Immigration Hypotheses in Western Europe' by Serge Feld (2000), concluded:

> It appears that only Italy will be faced with a fall in its working population. All other Western countries will either maintain the same level or, more generally, see their workforce grow substantially. Accordingly, we may safely assert that there is no risk of a shortage of workers between now and the year 2020, and that an increasing supply of labour will render reliance on a greater influx of immigrant workers unnecessary.

Indeed, the UK actually has the fastest growing labour force in Europe. According to *Labour Force Trends in the European Union and International Manpower Movements* (Serge Feld, 2001), the UK's labour force (using a tighter definition than the Government Actuary Service) will grow from 29,978,615 in 2000 to 30,985,138 in 2025, a larger expansion than any other country in the EU.

The Home Office is fully aware that there is no academic justification for the argument that immigration is necessary to combat a declining work force. In its study *International Migration and the United Kingdom: Recent Patterns and Trends*, it surveys the literature on the threat of a declining workforce, and concludes simply by quoting the *European Journal of Population*:

> Feld forecast that, with the exception of Italy, Western European countries as a whole will either maintain their working-age population at the existing level, or, more generally, see their workforce grow substantially up to the year 2020, largely as a

result of higher participation rates. Even under the least favourable scenarios, productivity gains more than compensate for any contraction in the working population.

However, this is clearly not the conclusion that the UK government has reached, although it has not given any demographic projections to justify its programme of rapidly accelerating the growth of the labour force through immigration.

It is likely that in the long term—after 2020—the UK workforce will start declining, although rising participation rates and productivity will mitigate the effects of it. There is widespread agreement on the need to end the culture of 'early exit', where the majority of men retire prematurely, and that childcare facilities should be increased to help women back to work, both of which will increase the actual number of people working. Retirement ages are also likely to rise, reflecting our increasingly lengthy healthy life expectancy and the need to pay for pensions (see chapter 12), and this too will have a dramatic effect on increasing the work force.

In addition, the EU is set to be enlarged to the East, which is a political imperative for reasons of stability and security in Europe, and will within a decade add countries with a population totalling 100 million to the European labour market. These countries are very low-income, with unemployment rates of up to 30 per cent providing an immense incentive for East Europeans to come to the West when free movement of labour is allowed. As well as Germany and Austria, a large number are likely to come to the UK, boosting the workforce without recourse to non-European immigration.

As before, if the workforce does start declining in a few decades time, and we want to reverse it, we can always quickly turn on the immigration tap then. But we do not need immigration to combat a declining workforce now.

6

Britain does not have a demographic time bomb

It is often said that Britain has a demographic time bomb, with the dwindling number of workers unable to support the growing numbers of elderly. It is certainly true that the numbers of elderly are growing, but it is not true that Britain has any sort of demographic time bomb—indeed quite the opposite over the next 20 years.

Once you take into account the rising retirement age of women to 65 by 2020, and the falling number of children, the ratio of people of working age to economic dependents actually falls over the next twenty years. According to the Government Actuary Service, the number of economic dependents per 1,000 people of working age will fall from 620 in 2000 to 583 by 2020. Only then does it start rising quite gently, and not at some catastrophic rate, and certainly far less than the sharp increases in the dependency ratio the UK has experienced and coped perfectly well with over the last century.

Table 4
Number of Dependents Per Thousand People of Working Age in the UK

Year	2000	2010	2020	2031	2040
Number of children and pensioners per 1,000 people of working age	620	609	583	698	755

Source: Government Actuary Service 2000-based projection, natural change only variant

When you then take into account rising levels of productivity and increasing participation of those of working age in the labour market, even the modest increase in the dependency ratio beyond the next 20 years actually poses no significant challenge.

These issues are dealt with in more depth in chapter 12.

7

How immigration has reached record levels

During the 1950s, the high immigration from the Commonwealth was largely balanced out by the emigration of British citizens, particularly to North America and Australia. Both emigration and immigration slowed as Britain and other countries tightened controls, but it remained reasonably in balance, with some net emigration during the 1970s and early 1980s.

However, during the '80s and '90s, while emigration grew again slowly, total immigration grew rapidly, from 153,000 in 1981 to slightly over 300,000 where it stayed throughout the 1990's until Labour was elected in 1997, after which it rapidly escalated to 482,000 in 2000.

This resulted in net immigration—the balance between people leaving and arriving—also growing rapidly, doubling between the early '90s and the late '90s. The net immigration of 183,400 in 2000 was the highest since records began, and the highest ever witnessed in Britain.

The acceleration of net immigration means that the total inflow more than quintupled from 157,000 between 1985 and 1990, to 837,000 between 1995 and 2000. It means that the net inflow added more than a million people to the population between 1992 and 2000.

The reason for the increase in immigration is not just the much commented-on growth in asylum. The number coming to the UK to both study and work has also roughly doubled, so that in 2000 it accounted for over 200,000 of the total inflow. This partly reflects government policy to make immigration easier across all categories, apart from asylum.

It abolished the 'primary purpose rule' so that now it is acceptable to marry for the primary purpose of immigrating to Britain. It now allows homosexuals to bring in their partners, and heterosexuals to bring in boyfriends of girlfriends who are married to other people, so long as they can show evidence of having been in a relationship for two years and living together for part of that time.

Table 5
Immigration and Emigration from the UK

Year	Inflow	Outflow	Balance
1981	153	233	-79
1982	202	259	-57
1983	202	185	17
1984	201	164	37
1985	232	174	59
1986	250	213	37
1987	212	210	2
1988	216	237	-21
1989	250	205	44
1990	267	231	36
1991	337	264	73
1992	287	252	35
1993	272	237	35
1994	321	213	109
1995	321	212	109
1996	331	238	93
1997	341	249	92
1998	402	224	178
1999	450	268	182
2000	482	299	183

Source: Office for National Statistics

It has rapidly increased temporary work permits from around 30,000 a year in the early '90s to 100,000 in 2001, and promised to increase this figure to 175,000 in 2002, while removing many of the restrictions on who they can be issued to. It has extended the holiday worker scheme, so people can come to the UK more than once and at older ages, and has tried to rebalance it so it isn't just Australians and New Zealanders, but also Africans and Asians (who are less likely to return home). It has embarked on a programme of massive recruitment of nurses from the Third World, bringing in 15,000 in 2001 alone. It has encouraged universities to recruit more students from overseas to generate more fees.

This and previous governments have also made it more difficult to deport people who are here illegally. The Conservatives abolished passport exit controls, ensuring that the government has no idea whether people are overstaying illegally or not. Labour introduced the Human Rights Act and applied it to immigration matters, thus making it almost impossible to deport illegal immigrants. It also gives anyone who has entered, either legally or illegally, the right to stay in the UK and receive free treatment for the rest of their lives on the NHS if they have a life-threatening condition such as HIV for which they cannot receive treatment in their home country.

Table 6
Reasons for Immigration to UK (thousands)

	All reasons	Work related	Joining spouse or family	Formal study	Other (inc asylum)
1991	337.0	52.3	99.1	61.1	124.5
1992	286.6	51.1	84.3	44.8	106.4
1993	272.2	49.8	80.8	51.9	89.6
1994	321.4	61.1	86.1	55.0	119.3
1995	320.7	60.8	67.1	67.2	125.6
1996	331.4	74.9	76.3	68.1	112.2
1997	340.7	67.8	80.0	92.8	100.0
1998	401.5	88.2	73.1	80.7	159.4
1999	450.0	96.1	85.4	84.9	183.5
2000	482.0	112.7	89.8	94.6	194.9

Source: Office for National Statistics

Obviously, many of the people who arrive leave a few years later, but the rise in immigration is not just simply a rise in the numbers of people coming and going—the number of people staying permanently has also risen sharply. The number of people given permission to settle in the UK remained below 60,000 a year in most of the 1980s and early 1990s, but has shown a dramatic jump since Labour came to power, increasing by almost 80 per cent from 69,790 in 1998 to 125,090 in 2000. This is largely the result of more refugees being granted permission to settle and more family reunions. Family reunions now count for around 70 per cent of those given permission to settle in the

UK, about 20 per cent relate to refugees and just seven per cent result from work or business.

Table 8
Reasons for Granting Permanent Settlement in UK

	1998	2000
Refugees	6,680	24,840
Children	12,280	28,990
Wives	22,290	30,920
Husbands	13,630	15,760
Other dependents (parents etc)	3,500	6,800
Work related reasons	4,210	6,130
Commonwealth citizen with UK grandparent	1,670	2,580
Other	5,530	9,070
Total	69,790	125,090

Source: Home Office

Most of the increase is because of higher settlements from low-income regions, namely Eastern Europe, Africa and Asia, of which the Indian sub-continent contributes about half. The largest rise is from Africa, which almost trebled its number of settlers to the UK in just two years, almost bringing it up to the level of Asia. The number of people settling from high-income regions such as North America and Australasia has increased more slowly, and so has declined as a proportion of the total. Whereas one in five settlers were from high-income countries (excluding the EU) in 1998, that had fallen to one in eight by 2000.

Table 9
Settlements Accepted by Region of Origin

Region	1998	2000
Eastern Europe	7,570	15,110
Americas	10,780	11,520
Africa	16,090	44,460
Asia	30,120	47,540
Australasia	3,690	4,900

Source: Home Office

The routes into the UK—through asylum, students, work visas and family reunion—may be different, but the pattern is the same. Although immigration flows are large with other high-income countries, they are balanced by emigration, and so don't affect overall population, and the migration flows are growing slowly. In contrast, migration from low-income countries is growing fast, largely one-way, and generally permanent—once in the UK, people rarely go back.

8

Why current immigration is different from previous waves of immigration

There is a trend in the voluminous canon of pro-immigration literature to suggest that what is happening now is just history as normal: migration, the ebb and flow of people, has always been a fact of life, and so should not be resisted. The culmination of this thesis is that Britain is a nation of immigrants, and so shouldn't resist further immigration.

Obviously, it is true that Britain is a nation of immigrants, as much as any nation on earth (apart from perhaps Tanzania, where man is thought to have evolved): people must have moved here at some point. In this sense it is as much a nation of immigrants as India, China, Saudi Arabia or Japan. This argument could also have been used to tell the aborigines in Australia that they shouldn't resist the white invasion.

However, Britain is not a nation of immigrants in the sense that immigration has not played a particularly significant role in the increase in population: almost the entire growth in population over the last thousand years has been through reproduction rather than net immigration. This is obviously in stark contrast to the white settler countries of the US, Canada, Australia or New Zealand, where immigration has played and continues to play a large part in population growth.

However, immigration now accounts for the majority of population growth in the UK, the first time this has happened in modern history. Previous waves of immigration in the last century have generally been one-off events of people genuinely fleeing persecution with a natural ending. However, what we have now for the first time is sustained large-scale one-way economically-driven immigration, with no end in sight (see chapter 9).

There were large, demographically significant waves of immigration before the Norman conquest. The Romans and Anglo-Saxons came over, transformed Britain and stayed. Most British people are to some extent descended from Romans or Anglo-Saxons and enjoy their influences—how can we object? This is the anaesthetic effect of the millennia.

However, our ancestors certainly objected, and sacrificed their lives in the effort; these early waves of immigration were bloody invasions that involved subjugation, mass killings and the destruction of cultures. Pro-immigrationists have a tendency to compare what is happening now to the invasion of the Romans, without mentioning that it led to years of bloody warfare, cultural obliteration and a country divided for centuries by walls mounted by fully armed soldiers. It is a comparison that you would expect the far Right to make.

More recent waves of immigration, which are often cited by pro-immigrationists, simply fail to compare to the level of immigration we are experiencing now.

About 50,000 Huguenots refugees were admitted after 1681, the equivalent to about three months worth of immigration now. They came to a smaller population, but we are accepting about four times that level of immigration every year, year in year out.

The number of Jews fleeing to Britain from Nazi persecution in the 1930s was 56,000, the equivalent of about three months immigration at current rates, but spread out over several years.

About 30,000 Asians came from Uganda in the early 1970s, forced out by General Idi Amin. We now get the equivalent of the East Asian immigration almost every six weeks.

There were no immigration controls on Commonwealth citizens until 1962, but the Home Office estimates the total intake between 1955 and 1962 was 472,000—a high level of immigration, but we are now experiencing levels of immigration about three times higher.

Pro-immigrationists often point out that in previous waves of immigration such as Huguenots, East Asian

Africans and Jews there was widespread unease about them at the time, but they are now judged a success—which indubitably they are.

However, there is an element here of picking winners. An honest assessment would also have to consider the impact of the Pakistani, Bangladeshi and West Indian immigrations, all of which have successes but are also associated with certain economic and social problems, and are probably not seen as obvious examples of success in the public mind.

The fact is that the Huguenot, Jewish and East African Asian immigrations were all successful because they were limited immigrations in scale and duration of highly educated and skilled people whose progeny integrated well. They were one-off events that had a natural conclusion.

The immigration now is completely different in degree and type. It is sustained, high-level immigration of groups, many of whom have lower level skills and education, who have generally suffered poorer employment outcomes, and some of whose progeny, we have learnt through harsh experience, are not integrating well.

9

Why it is one-way economically-driven large-scale immigration, with no end in sight

The ultimate reason for the record net immigration to the UK is that the UK is rich, much of the rest of the world is poor, and there are various ways that they can come here. Although the immigration routes include work permits, marriage, studying, asylum, clandestine entry or overstaying visas, the effect is the same: the record net immigration is a one way flow from the Third World to the UK.

As table 1 (p. 11) showed, people are far more likely to emigrate from the Third World to the UK than vice versa.

Nearly 12 times as many people emigrate from India, Bangladesh and Sri Lanka to the UK than vice versa, seven times as many from Pakistan, three times as many from the Caribbean, South Africa and other African Commonwealth countries. From the Middle East, the ratio of arrivals to departures is two to one. In contrast, with the developed world the migration is pretty evenly balanced, with equal numbers coming and going (with slight net emigration).

The result is that all the record net immigration to the UK is from the Third World and Eastern Europe, and that the flow is largely one way. It involves people emigrating from the poor world to the West to improve their lives.

The pattern is disguised by the various different routes of entry, but the consistent trend emerges of one-way immigration from poor countries to the UK, and balanced immigration with other rich countries.

The largest category of entry to the UK is family reunion—people bringing over spouses and children—and while this may be for love, it is such a large category for entry because people bring over their relatives from poor countries to the UK rather than vice versa. Almost 60,000 people were accepted for settlement last year from Africa and Asia for family reunion, but if there weren't an economic motivation, you would expect a large number of arranged marriages from India, say, to result in spouses moving from the UK to the subcontinent.

The same argument applies to asylum applications. Although they may be fleeing from somewhere, they are also fleeing to somewhere. Escaping from Afghanistan to Pakistan may be fleeing persecution; the secondary migration from Pakistan to the UK is then clearly economic migration that wouldn't have taken place if Pakistan had not been poor and Britain rich. Only around 10 per cent of asylum seekers to the UK have been found by the courts to be genuinely fleeing persecution, and the government has estimated that around 90 per cent of those claiming asylum paid people-smugglers to bring them to Britain. The British government has said that it thinks that the asylum flows to the UK are primarily economic in origin.

It is often said that immigrants often return home after a period of work, and indeed many do—particularly from the developed world. However, those from the Third World are clearly not that likely to return home, because the flows are so one-sided.

As table 10 (p. 32) shows, people from the Third World who arrive temporarily are far more likely to try to extend their stay, far more likely to get granted permanent settlement, and then far more likely to be granted UK citizenship. In contrast, the numbers from the developed world consistently fall away at each step of the process towards full UK citizenship.

Although people from the Americas (and particularly North America) are the most likely to enter on temporary work permits, they are unlikely to try to extend them. Although 33,800 entered on a temporary work permit last year, only 5,220 extended the work permit. This is because most are executives and managers within companies, who return to the US or Canada after a secondment or placement in the UK.

In contrast, the majority of workers from the Third World try to extend their work permits. Although 13,900 from India entered on a temporary work permit last year, 10,980 extended their work permit (they would have been people who entered in earlier years). Although 9,080 people from Africa entered the UK with temporary work permits, 7,490 extended them.

Nearly 41,000 out of the 91,800 temporary work permits issued last year went to people from Oceania and the Americas. However, they accounted for only about 7,850 of the 34,860 granted an extension to their work permit. They accounted for 16,420 out of the total of 125,090 granted the right to permanent settlement, and just 8,820 out of 90,295 granted UK citizenship in 2001 (and the largest group from the Americas was actually Jamaicans). In other words, immigrants from Americas and Oceania (including those from the West Indies) account for 44 per cent of temporary work permits, 23 per cent of work permit extensions, 13 per cent of those granted right to permanent settlement and 9.7 per cent of those granted full UK citizenship.

The official figures for citizenship (table 11 p. 33) are broken down in far more detail than those for settlement, and show the trend even more starkly. In 2001, more people from Mauritius became UK citizens than Canadians; more people from Ghana became UK citizens than people from the US, Canada, Australia and New Zealand combined.

Of the 90,295 people granted UK citizenship in 2001, only 5,915 came from the European Economic Area, North America, Oceania, Japan and South Korea. In other words, only seven per cent of those granted UK citizenship came from elsewhere in the developed world, and 93 per cent came from the Third World and Eastern Europe.

Given that the immigration is large-scale, one-way and economically driven from the Third World and Eastern Europe, it is unlikely to end until the economic imbalance disappears, or until there is a substantial reform of immigration policies.

There is an increase in wealth in countries such as India and China—although Africa is largely going backwards—but the disparities of wealth are so great that it is likely to be many decades before the economic incentive to migrate is eroded. A small upturn in unemployment in the UK may hit immigration from the developed world, but it will have less impact on immigration from countries where the average income is a tiny fraction of the UK average.

Similarly, the supply of potential immigrants will never dry up. There are a million Indians in Britain, but that is just 0.1 per cent of India's population of 1,029 million; there are 260,000 Bangladeshis in Britain but that is just 0.2 per cent of Bangladesh's population of 130 million; there are thought to be around one million Nigerians in Britain, but that is just 0.8 per cent of the total Nigerian population of 126 million.

Table 10
Work Permits, Settlement and Citizenship by Region of Origin

Region	Temporary work permit	Granted extension to work permit	Spouses and dependents accepted for settlement	Total granted right to permanent settlement	Granted Citizenship (2001)
EEA	0	0	0	0	1680
Americas	33,800	5,220	9,200	11,520	7,245
Rest of Europe	9,860	2,240	10,410	15,100	9,405
Africa	9,080	7,490	26,600	44,460	29,790
Indian subcontinent	13,900	10,980	20,340	22,730	23,745
Rest of Asia	17,900	6,210	14,530	24,810	11,725
Oceania	7,170	2,630	2,990	4,900	1,575
Other	100	100	860	1,560	0
Total	91,800	34,860	84,930	125,090	90,295

Source: Home Office, all for 2000 except citizenship

Table 11
Citizenship Granted in 2001

Country or Region of previous nationality	Passports granted (1997)	Passports granted (2001)	
EU and other EEA	**1,545**	**1,680**	
Other Europe	**2,785**	**9,405**	
of which: Turkey			4,050
Russia			790
Africa	**8,020**	**29,790**	
of which: Nigeria			6,290
Somalia			5,500
Ghana			3,195
South Africa			2,330
Sudan			1,270
Eritrea			1,255
Uganda			1,235
Kenya			1,040
Sierra Leone			845
Mauritius			775
India sub-continent	**8,456**	**23,745**	
of which: Pakistan			10,160
India			8,190
Bangladesh			5,395
Other Asia	**4,100**	**6,395**	
of which: Sri Lanka			2,770
China			1,590
Philippines			1,385
Thailand			815
Vietnam			590
South Korea			140
Japan			115
Middle East	**2,835**	**5,330**	
of which Iraq			1,835
Iran			1,450
Lebanon			775
Americas	**3,545**	**7,245**	
of which: Jamaica			2,070
United States			1,760
Canada			645
Trinidad and Tobago			520
Oceania	**1,445**	**1,575**	
of which New Zealand			825
Australia			615
TOTAL	**37,010**	**90,295**	

Source: Home Office

10

How record immigration has re-ignited population growth

The escalation of immigration has led to an unprecedented turn-around in the growth rate of the UK population, so that it was growing more than ten times faster in the late 1990s than it was in the late 1970s.

The natural growth of the population slowed during much of the twentieth century as fertility rates and the number of babies born steadily fell. By the 1970s, net emigration and a declining birth rate had actually stabilised the population for the first time since the industrial revolution. Between 1975 and 1978, and again in the recession of 1982, the population actually declined by a few tens of thousands of people.

However, from the mid-1980s onwards, fuelled by rising immigration, the population started growing again, and continued accelerating until the end of the century. While the population grew by an average of just under 70,000 a year in the 1970s, the growth rate had almost doubled to 124,000 a year in the 1980s. In the 1990s, it had almost doubled again, to grow by an average of 219,000 people a year. In the latter years of the 1990s, the population was growing by a quarter of a million people a year, or adding a city the size of Birmingham every five years. Overall, immigration has by itself added almost a million people to the UK population in just the last seven years.

After two decades of low or stable growth, the population was growing in 2000 at the fastest rate since the 1960s. For the first time in modern history, population growth is now fuelled almost entirely by immigration. Of the 255,000 increase in population in 2000, fully 183,000 came from immigration—in other words, the rise in immigration is quadrupling the natural rate of population growth.

Table 12
Five-Yearly Population Growth Rates in the UK

Year	Population (million)	Average annual growth in previous five years
1970	55.63	256,540
1975	56.23	118,700
1980	56.33	20,800
1985	56.69	72,600
1990	57.57	174,920
1995	58.61	208,880
2000	59.76	228,800

Source: Office for National Statistics

The accelerating level of immigration has caught population forecasters on the back foot, causing them to repeatedly underestimate the UK population in recent years.

The Office for National Statistics has repeatedly had to upgrade its forecasts. In 1999, it predicted that the UK population would be 62.2 million in 2021, and would peak at 63 million in 2031. In 2000, it forecast the population would be 63.6m by 2021, peaking at 65 million by 2036. In 2001, it forecast 65 million by 2025, and a peak of 66 million by 2040, or six million more people than at present.

Chris Shaw, the government actuary, said when he uprated the forecast: 'It's quite a big increase. The last two years since the previous projections have seen record numbers of migration. It has caused an unusual population increase.'

The 2001 census suggested there were one million fewer people in the UK than previously thought—largely because of one million missing men, whom the Office for National Statistics thought may be clubbing in Ibiza. In reality, the measured declines in population occurred in areas, such as Westminster, that have the largest transient populations, and lowest return rate of the forms. It is highly likely that the census just missed people, particularly illegal immigrants.

As mentioned in chapter 4, the scale of the impact of immigration on population growth can be seen by comparing the Government Actuary Service's different scenarios.

Assuming zero net immigration, the population will be 59.7m in 2031, whereas with migration at 195,000 a year—very similar to the levels we are experiencing—then the population will rocket to 68m by 2031, before rising to more than 70m by 2070. In other words, unless immigration falls from present levels it will mean that instead of stabilising at around 60m over the next 30 years, the UK population will accelerate to 70m.

Home Office ministers have said they want to see immigration of 150,000 a year, which would guarantee population growth for the next half century. However, the government has not said why it wants a growing population, nor given any indication of how it will decide that the population should stop growing at some point in the future.

11

How population growth damages the quality of life and the environment

The UK is already one of the most densely populated countries in the world, twice as densely populated as France, three times as densely populated as Spain, eight times as densely populated as America, and 70 times as densely populated as Canada. As table 13 (p. 40) shows, England itself is one of the most densely populated patches of land on the planet.

While there are relatively empty parts of the UK, the large majority of immigrants move to the area that is already the most densely populated, not only England, but the South East and London. This merely exacerbates the North/South divide in Britain, and does nothing to help the even development of the country or revitalise declining neighbourhoods in northern cities.

This high level of population density, which is rising almost entirely as a result of immigration, has severely negative impacts on many aspects of quality of life in Britain. It is bad for the environment and for the countryside, fuels the housing crisis and exacerbates traffic congestion. It was for these reasons that the Green Party used to campaign on the issue of population decline, arguing that the ideal population would be 30 million—until the rise of the immigration debate forced it to drop this proposal because it would appear to be 'immigrant bashing'. The British economy also suffers from congestion and land shortages.

In common parlance, Britain is full.

The South East of England, where most immigrants settle, has a population density very similar to that of the Netherlands, which the anti-immigration politician Pim Fortuyn declared was 'full'. Saying a country is full is often deemed a racist thing to say, but it is difficult to escape the conclusion that, however you define full, Britain, or at least the parts where immigrants move to, is also full.

You can tell Britain is full because it has no natural wilderness, and even its national parks not only have towns and villages in them, but actually have house-building programmes as well. Almost all of Britain's natural habitats, from the forests to its fenland, have been destroyed over the centuries to make room for people.

You can tell Britain is full because it is impossible to build another house, incinerator, asylum centre or even airport runway without local communities complaining bitterly about the impact it will have on them: there are no empty spaces left. The government has to behave in an authoritarian way and over-rule the wishes of local communities and force them to accept more housing, airports or asylum centres in their area.

The Joseph Rowntree Foundation said in a report that to avoid a housing crisis, Britain needs to build a million more homes in the next 20 years. This was probably an underestimate. According to the government's own housing projectionist, Dr David King, if immigration continues at the level that persisted between 1998 and 2000, of around 180,000 people a year, then it would be necessary to provide more than two million new homes just for immigrants by 2021.

The Mayor of London has said that London needs houses for another 700,000 people by 2014, all of whom would be immigrants, because British people are leaving London. There is increasing pressure to open up the beloved greenbelts that encircle cities to create room for more housing. The Mayor of London, and others in the pro-immigration lobby, suggest that Britain has too low density housing, and must accept greater density housing. In other words, to accommodate the record levels of immigration, the people already living here must accept the need to live in smaller houses with smaller gardens to make room for newcomers.

Population growth and shortage of housing also pushes up house prices to levels at which first-time buyers and key workers such as nurses and teachers find them almost unaffordable. After the government increased its projections for immigration from 95,000 a year to 135,000 a year, the Centre for Economic and Business Research dramatically upgraded its projections for house price growth in London, declaring the pressure on housing was such that prices would treble in the next 20 years.

Immigration is now a greater source of household creation than that of natural population growth, and the increasing desire of people to live on their own rather than co-habit. The Joseph Rowntree Foundation says that immigration only amounts to 20 per cent of the new demand for housing because immigrants tend to live in smaller houses with larger households. But that misses the long-term impact—as the immigrants and their descendants integrate and become richer, they will have the same housing needs as the native population.

You can tell London is full because train stations such as Kings Cross occasionally have to close for safety reasons because the crowds are too big; because underground stations close on a daily basis because the overcrowding is dangerous; because in rush hour underground trains are so full that commuters simply can't get on them and have to wait for several to pass. The government can improve public transport, but the immigration-fuelled population growth is happening well before any such improvements in infrastructure are seen.

There is constant congestion on the roads, and the M25 is often little more than a car park. Road space is so short that people have to pay residents' parking fees for permission to park their car, but even then are not guaranteed a space. During the Christmas season, central shopping areas in London become so crowded that police have to erect barricades to stop pedestrians entering. Hospitals are so packed that patients have to routinely wait six hours in accident and emergency. Patients have to wait up to two weeks just to see their GP. Schools in many towns are full to bursting point.

All these quality of life issues are of concern to people who already live in Britain, and all are likely to get worse as a result of population growth.

Table 13
Population Densities of Selected Countries

Country	Population Density (people per sq km)	Population Density (UK=1)	Land Area (sq km)	Population (m)
Netherlands	471.7	1.91	33,883	15,981,472
England	386.5	1.56	129,365	49,997,000
India	346.4	1.40	2,973,190	1,029,991,145
United Kingdom	246.9	1.00	241,590	59,647,790
Germany	237.8	0.96	349,223	83,029,536
Italy	196.2	0.79	294,020	57,679,825
China	136.5	0.55	9,326,410	1,273,111,290
France	109.1	0.44	545,630	59,551,227
Spain	80.1	0.32	499,542	40,037,995
Ireland	55.8	0.22	68,890	3,840,838
USA	30.4	0.12	9,158,960	278,058,881
New Zealand	14.4	0.058	268,670	3,864,129
Russia	8.56	0.035	16,995,800	145,470,197
Canada	3.43	0.014	9,220,970	3,592,805
Australia	2.54	0.010	7,617,930	19,357,594

Source: *Central Intelligence Agency World Fact Book 200*, Office for National Statistics

12

Why immigration is not a 'fix' for an ageing population

The most beguiling and one of the most often repeated arguments is that we need immigration to compensate for an ageing society and the rise in the number of pensioners. Government ministers, race campaigners, university professors and almost every newspaper pundit tell us that we need to import the surplus young workers of the developing world to care for the growing ranks of the elderly in the developed world, and create the wealth to pay for our pensions. This is the idea of 'replacement migration'.

There is only one problem. This argument is one of the most widespread and comforting self-delusions since humanity believed the sun went around the earth. It is the triumph of wishful thinking and the attractiveness of a neat idea over elementary demographics: immigrants are no fix for an ageing society because they age too.

It is an idea that is fundamentally flawed, and has been discredited by every authority that has looked at it, including the United Nations, the Council of Europe, the European Commission, the UK's Government Advisory Service, the Home Office and the Organisation for Economic Co-operation and Development. Those who continue to punt this notion are either ignorant or wilfully dishonest.

Home Office civil servants are clearly frustrated that this idea, having been so totally and utterly discredited, is still given such wide circulation by those who wish to promote immigration. The introduction of the Home Office's report *International Migration and the United Kingdom: Patterns and Trends* (2001) says:

> The impact of immigration in mitigating population ageing is widely acknowledged to be small because immigrants also age. For a substantial effect, net inflows of migrants would not only need to occur on an annual basis, but would have to rise continuously. Despite these and other findings, debate about the link between changing demography and a migration 'fix' refuses to go away.

The UK government actuary Chris Shaw did a comprehensive analysis of the effect of a range of different levels of immigration on the ageing of the population, and wrote up his conclusions in *Population Trends* in Spring 2001:

> Despite much recent attention being focused on migration, it is clear that this is not a long term solution to the 'problem' of population ageing.

The Organisation for Economic Co-operation and Development, in its 2001 study *Trends in Immigration and Economic Consequences*, was more diplomatic in its conclusions:

> While immigration can partly offset slower growing or declining OECD populations, it cannot provide by itself a solution to the budgetary implications of ageing populations.

The Council of Europe in its study *Europe's Population and Labour Market Beyond 2000*, concluded:

> Migration flows cannot in future be used to reverse trends in population ageing and decline in most Council of Europe countries. The flows required would be too large and it would be impossible to integrate them into the economy and society. Such a policy would also require a sort of 'fine tuning' of the flows by age and gender which would be discriminatory and very difficult to manage.

Even the United Nations report *Replacement Migration: is it a Solution to Declining and Ageing Population?* which is so often cited as proving the case for replacement migration, actually concluded the complete opposite. Although the authors of the UN report were clearly keen to prove the case for replacement migration, they reluctantly conclude that the scale of migration needed to change the demographic profile of a whole country is so large as to be 'out of reach'. To get an idea of how large, take the example of how much replacement migration would be needed to combat the effect of ageing in South Korea (one of the most rapidly ageing societies on earth): almost the entire population of the earth would have to emigrate to South Korea by 2050. This is not scaremongering, but the UN Population Division's own forecast.

The truth is that replacement migration is a short-term fix for a challenge that makes things far worse in the long run, and so is a massive betrayal of our children.

The trouble with the UK importing young people is that they grow older and retire themselves, meaning that the UK would then need to import more young people to look after them, putting the UK on an escalator of perpetually and exponentially growing population that it has to get off at some point. The only long-term way to avoid an ageing society, should you want to, is to kill people or force them to emigrate at a certain age (see chapter 13).

Key to the issue is the 'dependency ratio', which the UN defines as the ratio between the number of people of working age compared to the number of pensioners. At the moment, this ratio is 4.09:1 in the UK, but in the absence of immigration, changes in fertility and retirement age, it is forecast to decline to 2.5:1 by 2050. It has been widely argued that 2.5 workers simply aren't enough to care for and pay the pension and healthcare costs of each retired person—the burden would be just too great.

Hence, bring in the young people. But if you want to keep the support ratio at four to one, and you import a million young people, then, when they retire, you would need to import four million young people to support them. When those four million retire, you would need to import 16 million to support them, and so on.

In his report in *Population Trends*, the government actuary Chris Shaw put it like this:

> The single reason why even large constant net migration flows would not prevent support ratios from falling in the long term is that migrants grow old as well! Although a steady large inflow of young migrants would continue to boost the working-age population, before long it would also start adding to the retirement-age population, and a four-to-one (say) potential support ratio could not be maintained.

The UN calculates that to keep the UK dependency ratio at 4.09:1, the UK would need to have 59,775,000 immigrants by 2050, increasing the population to 136 million. At the end of that period, immigration would need to be running at 2.2 million a year, and still growing exponentially. To carry on this strategy of replacement migration, the UK would then need to import about another 130 million by 2100, doubling the population to about a quarter of a billion.

And that is the key point: if we follow the replacement migration strategy, then at 2050 we would be left with exactly the same challenge now of adjusting to an ageing society, but with twice the population.

Table 14
Replacement Migration needed to keep Ratio of Pensioners and Working Population Constant until 2050

Country or Region	Average annual migration	Total immigration by 2050
France	1,792,000	89,584,000
Germany	3,630,000	181,508,000
Italy	2,268,000	113,381,000
Japan	10,471,000	523,543,000
Republic of Korea	102,563,000	5,128,147,000
Russian Federation	5,068,000	253,379,000
United Kingdom	1,194,000	59,722,000
United States	11,851,000	592,572,000
Europe	27,139,000	1,356,932,000
European Union	13,480,000	673,999,000

Source: *Replacement Migration: is it a Solution to Declining and Ageing Population?*, United Nations Population Division

The scale of immigration needed to avoid adapting to an ageing society is extraordinary, as table 14 shows; what it doesn't show is that it is exponential and never reaches a plateau, it just keeps on growing. The US and Japan would need half a billion immigrants each, but they will then still be facing the same problem.

Somehow, the pro-immigration lobby see this as a feasible strategy, and repeatedly quote the UN report. But the UN's report, far from endorsing it, actually just asked the questions in the title, and then concluded:

> Maintaining potential support ratios at current levels through replacement migration alone seems out of reach, because of the extraordinarily large numbers of migrants that would be required.

The question then is, what about a little bit of migration to soften the ageing of society, slowing down the transition? If it is not possible to maintain support ratios at four-to-one in the UK, perhaps some immigration can stop it falling all the way to 2.5? Because of the scale of migration needed to alter the demographic profile of a nation of 60 million people, anything that is in the bounds of political or practical reality will have very little effect indeed.

According to the UN's calculations, if the UK had no immigration and all other things being equal, the support ratio would fall to 2.36:1 by 2050. Letting in 124,000 immigrants every year only raises the support ratio to 2.64:1.

Table 15
Effect of Immigration on Support Ratio

Average annual immigration	Total immigration by 2050	Support ratio by 2050
0	0	2.36
24,000	1.2m	2.37
52,000	2.6m	2.49
124,000	6.2m	2.64
1,196,000	59.8m	4.09

Source: *Replacement Migration: is it a Solution to Declining and Ageing Population?*, United Nations Population Division

The government actuary Chris Shaw reached the same conclusion in *Population Trends*:

> The support ratio is set to decline under any plausible set of future assumptions. So, maintaining the support ratio at the current level is a wholly unrealistic scenario.

Obviously, immigration leads to some improvement in the support ratio in the short term, but the change is pretty negligible compared to the scale of the immigration. And nor does it answer the point of what you do at 2050—you will have to carry on the immigration at increasingly high levels to permanently keep the support ratio that low.

According to Chris Shaw, to maintain a support ratio of just 3.23 in 2050, the UK would need to import a million immigrants a year. He told *The Times* (15 November 2001): 'Very high migration scenarios clearly demonstrate that, although they would provide a short-term boost to support ratios, even massive net migration inflows would not prevent support ratios from ultimately falling'.

The Council of Europe is unequivocal that it is a mistake for governments to try and engineer the demographics of their country through immigration, concluding:

> Immigration policies should be governed by political and humanitarian objectives, and not by demographic considerations.

In fact, there are many long-term ways of improving the real support ratio, without resorting to the short-term fix of immigration. The UN only looks at the support ratio in terms of people of working age and people of pensionable age, which is just one demographic ratio of little relevance to the real world. In fact, there are other groups of dependents, and there are many other simple ways to increase the actual number of people working, such as raising participation rates and retirement ages and reducing unemployment.

Children are also dependents who cost money and don't earn, and just as the number of pensioners grows, so the number of children is set to decline, and the total dependency ratio of workers to dependents is far more benign. In fact, as shown in chapter 6, the Government Actuary Service predicts that once you include the impact of children and the rising retirement age of women, the overall dependency ratio actually improves over the next 20 years, from 620 dependents per 1,000 people of working age now to 583 dependents per 1,000 people of working age in 2020.

Even this ignores the fact that actually many people of working age don't work. Taking into account people actually working versus those dependent on them gives you the 'real support ratio', where the trend is even more benign. There is almost certainly going to be higher participation in the labour market, as parents and particularly women are successful in getting more family-friendly employment, and as people live longer and healthier lives, refusing to give up work at 55. The raising of women's retirement age to 65 by 2020 will also have a very positive impact on the support ratio.

Productivity—basically the amount of wealth created by an hour's work—also increases by an average of over two per cent per year because of improving technology and efficiency. This increase in productivity makes it steadily easier for workers to generate the wealth to look after the elderly.

The government actuary Chris Shaw wrote in *Population Trends Spring 2001*:

> measures such as raising workforce participation rates or discouraging early retirement are likely to remain a more practical tool for increasing the working population than attempting to influence demographic behaviour.

In addition to all this is the effect of fertility levels on the support ratio, which turn out to be quite large. In fact, the government actuary showed in *Population Trends* that if fertility were to rise, it would be far more potent than immigration as a long-term method of sustainably raising the support ratio without sparking large population growth:

> Interestingly, a long-term TFR of 2.0 children per woman would produce much the same support ratio at 2100 as would annual net migration of half-a-million people a year, but with a total population of 75 million rather than 120 million ... higher fertility levels, if they could be achieved, would produce markedly higher long-term support ratios.

13

Why an ageing society is inevitable for the UK and the rest of the world

There is a widespread perception, perhaps encouraged by reports such as the United Nations' *Replacement Migration: is it a Solution to Declining and Ageing Population?*, that an ageing society is something that can somehow be 'solved', in the sense of keeping the average age of the society low, and reducing the ratio of old people to young people.

However, an ageing society is the logically inevitable consequence of increasing life expectancies and stabilising populations. It can only be avoided by reducing life expectancies or ensuring a perpetually exponentially growing population.

The proportion of young people can be increased through immigration or raised birth rates, but since today's youngsters are tomorrow's pensioners, that means a perpetually growing population to keep that proportion up. Or it can be avoided by reducing the number of old, which means culling them at a certain age, or exiling them overseas.

Since the former is unsustainable in the long run (the population must stop growing at some point; we cannot have an infinite number of people), and the latter is politically unacceptable, we have to accept that an ageing society is inevitable. There is in the long run no other option; any other policies are just an attempt to postpone the inevitable.

It is not just inevitable for the West, but for the whole world: the populations of all countries must stop growing at some point, and the advantages of public health improvements and medical science are increasing life expectancies almost everywhere (the exceptions being the tragic cases of Southern African countries where AIDS is reducing life expectancies).

The rich countries of the world—in particular Europe and Japan—got there first, but almost all other countries including India, China and Brazil are following. If an ageing society is a disaster that can only be solved by rich countries importing young people from poor countries, it doesn't portend well for mankind. When the whole of the earth reaches the phase that the West is in now, what do we do? Start an immigration programme from Mars?

An ageing society is just the latest—and quite probably the ultimate—demographic phase of humankind. For most of history, humanity has had high mortality and high fertility, keeping the population stable with a low life expectancy. There was a time lag between declines in mortality and declines in fertility, which meant that fewer people died than were born and populations exploded. Finally, fertility declines also, ensuring a stable population with high life expectancy—and that inevitably means a higher average age and higher ratio of old people to young people.

An ageing society is not something we can escape, but it is something we can adjust to.

14

Why health care will be affordable in an ageing society

Many people are frightened of an ageing society because they believe it will not be able to afford its healthcare costs. They foresee the army of frail elderly sending hospital bills into orbit, and the country unable to afford the armies of doctors and gerontologists that the old are demanding.

Despite being common sense, this misunderstands the nature of healthcare costs and its relationship with ageing, and the nature of health supply and demand. In fact, studies on the subject show that the impact of an ageing society on health spending will be relatively small. This is because the effect of increasing life expectancy is not so much to increase healthcare costs, but to postpone them.

Life expectancy is increasing, but so is healthy life expectancy, although not at the same rate. However, there is strong evidence from the US and UK that there have been substantial declines in severe disability with age.

Around a quarter of healthcare costs are incurred in the last year of life, but the cost of that last year of life does not increase with age, but appears to fall. A study by NHS Scotland ('Proximity to death and acute healthcare utilisation in Scotland'), suggests that if someone dies in their seventies, the cost in the last year of their life is about £5,000 whereas, if it is in their eighties, it is £4,000.

The Wanless Report into the future of healthcare spending for the Treasury, concluded:

> Demographic changes have had less of an impact on health spending than many people tend to think. There is a widening body of evidence which shows that proximity to death has a larger impact on health care costs than age. It is therefore possible that the effect of an ageing population will be to postpone rather than increase health service costs. Previous studies have suggested that demographic change will add less than 1 per cent a year to costs. If ageing postpones costs, the impact on costs could be lower.

In any case, health care always has been and always will be simply a matter of what we can afford. We have to ration health care now, denying certain treatments to some patients, and under all feasible future scenarios—whether there is immigration or not—we will have to continue rationing health care in the future.

Aside from demographic factors, healthcare costs rise above inflation because technology advances, and high technology generally (but not always) costs more than low technology. But this increasing cost of health care is simply a reflection of the fact that we are getting better and better health care. In all nations, health systems cannot afford to give everyone the latest technology all the time, and again there is rationing. But even so, the standard of health care and health outcomes is continuously rising for almost all people in the West.

Healthcare costs are likely to continue rising as a proportion of GDP as society gives more importance to maintaining health. But a rise in healthcare costs is certainly no reason to panic, or to start a massive immigration programme. It is almost certain that the richest, longest living, most productive society the earth has ever seen with the highest level of medical technology the world has ever seen will get far better health care than we do now.

15

Why we should welcome an ageing society

The prospect of an ageing society fills many otherwise rational people with dread. They worry about a greying world, a stagnant place bereft of youthful vigour with unsupportable numbers of dribbling pensioners packing out care homes on every street corner, bleeding the small number of workers dry of every penny of wealth they slave away to generate.

If you suffer this fear, you've been reading too many newspapers. It is just ageist hysteria.

People will be living longer than ever before, with longer, healthier working lives than ever before, more educated, more affluent, with more experience, higher productivity, and better technology than ever before. This is the most powerful society the earth has ever seen. And yet, perversely, we are lead to believe this is just about the first society in history that is incapable of supporting itself.

An ageing society is nothing to be frightened of. It is the ultimate phase in the development of humanity, the triumph of our struggling over the centuries to make the most of our lives and make a better world. The increase in life expectancy of most societies over the last century—unprecedented in history and across any species—is the single most successful act of collective endeavour that this planet has ever witnessed. Everyone wants to live long and healthy lives, and we're achieving it. Rejoice!

People are frightened of an ageing society because it is a step into the unknown, and because we have a youth-obsessed culture and ageist prejudices. But almost all our fears about it are totally unfounded.

It won't be a world of bored, inert wrinklies. As people expect to live longer, they just spread their lives out. If you think you will die at 40, you pack it all in quickly. When we know we have 80 years we act like teenagers into our twenties, start families in our thirties, and then start playing again when the kids have left and we have time, money and energy. The most rapidly growing area of adventure holidays is for the over-sixties. This isn't an old society, it is a society of permayouth. People are clubbing and taking ecstasy into their thirties and beyond, once youthful rockers are touring into their fifties. People who retired at 55 are going back to work at 65 because they are fit and healthy and full of beans.

More and more people are working into their seventies and beyond. The decline of manual labour, and the rise of the 'knowledge worker' means both that work is far more rewarding now than it used to be, and that it is far more doable by people past their physical but not intellectual prime.

Judges don't retire until they are 70, and politicians, actors and writers often carry on pretty much until they die. Churchill ran the country in his eighties, John Gielgud acted into his nineties, Rupert Murdoch is running one of the world's largest media groups in his seventies, Lord Deedes is still working as a foreign correspondent in his eighties and Alan Greenspan is the world's most powerful and respected central banker even though he is in his late seventies. The Queen Mother insisted on working until she was a hundred years of age, and her daughter is still an active head of state in her seventies.

We are going through a demographic transition from a younger, growing population to an older, stable one, and that will require adjustments. Institutions and practices that depend on a growing population and short life expectancy will have to adapt. The pension system will have to go from a pay-as-you-go system where today's taxpayers pay today's pensioners to a funded one, where people save up during their lives to pay for their retirement.

Companies will no longer be able to afford to throw people on the scrap heap at 55 so they can bring in the young ones. At present older people don't have the latest skills, because virtually no companies train anyone over 40. Yet studies show those in their fifties are as capable of learning new techniques as people in their twenties. We have to ditch the culture of early exit, which means that only a third of men work to the retirement age, and combat corporate ageism. Companies such as Sainsbury's and B&Q are already discovering the joys of older workers: they have far more experience, they are far more stable, and they are far more reliable.

The retirement age of 65 was the invention of a time when few people lived healthily beyond that, but now most people live healthily into their seventies and beyond. The retirement age will have to be raised, or simply abolished altogether: everyone should be able to choose when they stop, so long as they can afford to do so. No one who actually enjoys work should be forced to retire when they can carry on being productive.

Having longer, healthier, productive lives means we can generate more wealth during our lives, not less, and so pay for pensions. There is simply no evidence that we will not be able to afford the health bills or pensions for an ageing society.

The Council of Europe in its 2001 study *Europe's Population and Labour Market Beyond 2000* concluded that the ageing workforce would be an economic boon rather than a burden:

> Fears that an ageing employed workforce could negatively affect productivity and the capacity to adapt to technical change have been largely unfounded. An ageing workforce could certainly require adaptions in training methods and personnel management policies at the level of the firm. Older workers, however, tend to be highly motivated and, in many respects, they can be more productive and flexible than younger ones. The higher employment rates of these groups will not, therefore, detract from the competitiveness of productive systems. On the other hand, this is a trait that should be strongly encouraged both for the well-being of the individuals involved and to reduce the menaces that ageing populations can pose for social expenditure and for the financial viability of pension systems and the cost of health care.

An older society will have many advantages a younger one doesn't. It will have less crime, since most crime is committed by the young. It will be more politically stable, since the old, with the collected wisdom of a lifetime, don't do revolutions. As Kofi Annan, secretary general of the United Nations, said:

> Trees grow stronger over the years, rivers wider. Likewise, with age, human beings gain immeasurable depth and breadth of experience and wisdom. That is why older people should be not only respected and revered; they should be utilised as the rich resource to society that they are.

We have to give up our addiction to a growing, youthful population and welcome the golden olden era. An older society is a mature, confident, wise, highly educated, highly skilled society where everyone lives their lives to the full. It is the pinnacle of human development. Rejoice! We should adapt to it and welcome it, not try and prevent it with immigration.

16

Why Europe's low fertility is set to bounce back up

The demographic transition from high fertility and high mortality to low fertility and low mortality that is sweeping the entire world hit its latest—and to some people scariest—stage in the Baltic republics in the 1950s. For the first time, women apparently started having too few babies to replace themselves. The technical measurement of fertility, known as Total Fertility Rate (TFR), dropped below the replacement rate of 2.01, the minimum number of babies needed for the population to remain stable.

Much of the rest of the developed world followed, starting in Scandinavia and sweeping through Belgium and Netherlands to France and Italy and Greece, taking in Japan and Australia, and followed most recently by China and Thailand. More than 60 countries now have below-replacement fertility, and the TFR has just carried on falling with no sign of stopping. In Britain it fell below 1.7 in 2002, and in parts of Southern Europe it has dropped to just over one. Many women are just not having babies at all – in Britain the number of women who will never have children has risen to one in five, the highest level of childlessness in a peacetime generation. Women are too busy working and having fun to have babies, it seems.

From baby boom to birth dearth in just a few decades, and the stories started appearing that the modern world was about to die out.

With fewer births than deaths each year, there were endless predictions that the population was set to go into freefall, with horrible accounts of the devastating economic and social effects. There is only one thing worse than a booming population, it was said, and that is a declining—and ageing—population. The Japanese government even calculated that within 1,500 years the country would have only one person left. The Japanese race would have a lonely lingering death.

It makes for perfect newspaper scare stories, some of which I have written myself, but it should not be used to inform policy. There is only one thing wrong with the scenario: the real world. Scratch under the surface, and the situation is far more subtle and far less worrying.

The figures for TFR—an artificial mathematical construction—greatly understate the West's real level of fertility. Most demographers—including those at the UN—believe that nothing worse will happen than a temporary undershooting of the fertility rate, before it rises again to its natural equilibrium point, the replacement rate. In those countries furthest ahead on the demographic curve—such as Denmark and Finland—fertility is already rising.

The Total Period Fertility Rate is a very volatile measure that vastly understates of the level of fertility during times of transition when women are delaying having babies. It is a snapshot at a particular time, a highly artificial mathematical construction of an average fertility from the fertility rates of women at different ages of their life at that particular time: i.e. if a woman went through life with the levels of fertility pertaining at that moment then that is the number of children she would end up having. Because it takes the fertility rates of a snapshot in time and extrapolates them over a lifetime it is only accurate if society's fertility rates remain stable over the lifetime.

But fertility rates go up and down, and TFR greatly exaggerates the swings. While we are in a time when women are still delaying babies to a later and later age, it will vastly understate the level of fertility. Likewise, when the trend to later babies stops—as it must do at some point —then it will overshoot the other way.

TFR also doesn't reflect the fact that there is still a lot of demographic momentum with more people of child-bearing age than we would have in an equilibrium state ensuring that the population is still growing. Even though the TFR measurement is down to a historic low of 1.64, the UK still has more babies than deaths each year, ensuring natural population growth. In fact, despite concerns about Britain not having enough babies, the echoes of the baby boom ensure that more babies are born each year in the late 1990s than in the late 1970s.

A different measure of fertility, cohort fertility, measures the actual number of babies that a woman could expect to have by the end of her reproductive life, taking account of the changing fertility rates throughout her life, and this fertility rate is much higher. In France in 1995, the TFR was 1.7, but cohort fertility was 2.2—above replacement level. In the Netherlands in 1995, TFR was 1.5, but the cohort fertility was a very respectable 1.9.

It is not just the result of the intrinsic mathematics of TFR that will see that fertility will rise again, but the attitudes of adults. There is very little evidence that women —or their partners—are actually going off babies. Surveys have consistently shown that women in Europe want more than two babies. In the UK, more than a half of women want two babies, and a third want more than three. On average, British women want 2.4 babies each—well above replacement rate.

Table 16
2002: Number of Babies desired by British Women

Number of babies	0	1	2	3	4	5 or more
% wanting	8.4	3.6	55.0	13.9	13.9	5.3

Source: *Population Trends Summer 2002*, Office for National Statistics

The reason for the low fertility is not that women don't want babies, but that they are having fewer babies than they want. However, that is partly a reflection of the fact we have just gone through a rapid process of women getting involved in the paid workforce and developing careers, and in the headlong rush many aspects of childrearing—such as the provision of childcare facilities, family-friendly working practices and the need not to leave it too late—have been left behind. There is no reason to believe that women—richer, more successful and with more freedoms than ever before—will persistently be denied such a fundamental fulfilment as having the number of babies they actually want.

As has been well documented in books like *Baby Hunger* by Sylvia Ann Hewlett, the first generation of 'have-it-all women' often ended up childless by mistake—they left it late and just didn't realise how fast their fertility declined in their 30s. The second generation of such women are likely to learn from the first about the dangers of leaving it too late.

For a variety of reasons, there is almost certain to be a continuing increase in childcare provision and facilities such as crèches at work, and a far more mature attitude among companies to family-friendly working. This will make it far easier for women to combine work and babies. Fertility treatments are improving all the time, at a quite remarkable rate, and are likely to get far more widespread in usage and far more successful (as we are already seeing with IVF). Many couples who in the past would have had to resign themselves to childlessness will not have to in the future.

Also, if the birth dearth is a national concern, then it is relatively simple for governments to pursue pro-natalist policies, encouraging people to have more babies by giving increasing financial incentives, giving more time off work for both parents and so on. Such policies can be justified not on demographic grounds but simply because it is a legitimate aim of social policy to enable people to have the number of babies they want.

This is the route pursued by Scandinavian countries. The report of a 1997 UN expert group meeting on below replacement fertility stated:

> The Nordic countries, in pa.ticular in Sweden and Norway, fertility substantially increased in the late 1980s and approached or even surpassed the replacement level. This reversal of fertility decline may have been associated with large-scale social policies aimed at creating conditions (through significantly extending childcare facilities, and increasing family allowances) which allow women to combine professional careers with motherhood.

There are also many theoretical reasons to assume that fertility will rise again to the replacement rate. The 1997 UN report states:

> Intrinsically, the 'magnetic force' toward replacement (Westoff, 1991) is based on the homeostatic argument of the demographic transition theory: an initial equilibrium between high birth rates and high death rates is disturbed by declining mortality which in turn triggers a fertility decline that brings birth and death rates back to an equilibrium at low levels. Most explicitly developed by Vishnevsky (1976,1991), the homeostasis argument suggests that fertility levels ultimately result from the development of the 'demographic system' that aims at its own inherent goals of self-maintenance and survival, rather than are the sum of individual behaviour. Fertility levels that dropped substantially below replacement levels or stayed below replacement for relatively long time are construed as aberrations or overshootings that will be inevitably reversed in the future.

Far from Britain and Europe dying out from lack of babies, most demographers and the UN itself believe that there will only be a temporary undershooting of fertility, lasting perhaps a few decades. During that time population may decline slightly, but it will then stabilise at a slightly lower level (no bad thing in a country as crowded as the UK).

There is no need for immigration now—which is permanent—to make up for a transient shortfall in babies. As always, if fertility doesn't come back up and population decline does become severe—perhaps in 30 years time—then it will be easy to turn the immigration tap on at that time. But there is absolutely no reason to try and pre-empt this by adopting policies of large-scale immigration in the early years of the twenty-first century that simply quadruple the population growth rate.

Ironically, one of the policies that could prevent the fertility rates of British women bouncing back up is large-scale immigration. Extensive research shows that people have more babies when they are more positive about the future, and when they have the right conditions in terms of housing and employment. The impact of immigration on native fertility is likely to be greater in a country already suffering from overcrowding such as the UK than in a far emptier country such as the United States.

By making access to decent housing more difficult, immigration could indirectly lead to native women having fewer babies. By boosting the population, high immigration exacerbates the housing crisis, leads to a shortage of social housing, and increases pressure for people to live in small houses or flats. The Council of Mortgage Lenders claims (*The Times*, 3 July 2002) that immigration is largely responsible for the consistent rise in house prices above average earnings, while research from the Economic and Social Research Council shows that house prices are so high and access to decent housing so difficult that couples put off getting married and one in three put off having babies. It concluded that high house prices would lead to women having fewer babies (*Evening Standard*, 17 September 2002).

By increasing the supply of cheap labour with low expectations, high immigration may not only reduce the job prospects of people in the UK, but provides less incentive for companies to introduce genuine family-friendly working, which in turn is likely to discourage some women having babies.

Problems with overstretched schools and health services could also only discourage British women from having babies. If immigration leads to increased social tension, then that would also discourage women from having babies by increasing uncertainty about the future.

17

Why there are no labour shortages in Europe or the UK

One of the most common justifications for immigration is that there are labour shortages in Europe, a startling contention given that there are 13.4 million unemployed in the European Union, according to the European Commission. There are over four million unemployed in Germany, and unemployment in Spain is over 11 per cent. In every major European economy apart from the UK, unemployment is over eight per cent, an historically very high rate. In addition, it is the most vulnerable who suffer the highest unemployment—the young, women, the unskilled, ethnic minorities and recent immigrants.

In 1997, when unemployment in Germany was the highest it had been since Hitler came to power, European governments and other industrial nations put out statements saying that unemployment—in effect, too much labour and not enough jobs—was the biggest problem facing modern industrialised society. Just five years later, unemployment has fallen only slightly, but pro-immigration pressure groups are proclaiming that labour shortages and too many jobs are the biggest problem facing modern industrialised economies.

In the UK, unemployment is comparatively low at 5.1 per cent, according to the Labour Force Survey definition, which is widely regarded as the most reliable (the claimant count is just an administrative measure of how many people are out of work and claiming benefits). However, that still means that there are 1.55 million people unemployed in the UK. In addition to this there are 2.3 million people who aren't working but say they would like to work, but don't count as officially unemployed because they are not actively seeking jobs—they are generally discouraged workers such as women with children who don't think any job will pay for childcare costs, or prematurely retired men. In total, there are nearly four million people in the UK who don't have a job but want one.

The UK is now part of a single labour market with 13.4 million unemployed. However, the labour surpluses in the EU will get even more stark when the EU expands East, taking in countries with unemployment rates of up to 30 per cent.

Table 17
Unemployment in Major European Economies

Region or category	Unemployment rate (%)
Spain	11.4
France	9.2
Italy	9.0
Germany	8.1
UK	5.1
European Union	7.6
EU men	6.7
EU women	8.7
EU under 25 year olds	16.5

Source: *Eurostat*, June 2002

There may be specific skills shortages—such as cardiac surgeons—in which case we should certainly bring them in, which is exactly what the government is doing. Companies have also always been free to get work permits for non-EU workers if they cannot find an appropriate one in the EU.

But there are not generalised labour shortages in Europe, or the UK—particularly not unskilled labour shortages. The unskilled are four times as likely to be unemployed as the skilled. Ethnic minorities in Britain are twice as likely to be unemployed as white people, with some communities such as Pakistanis and Bangladeshis suffering unemployment of around 50 per cent.

It is, of course, quite possible to have a surplus of unskilled and semi-skilled labour at the same time as having a labour shortage, if the types of jobs are not appropriate for those who are out of work. It may be difficult to get an unemployed coal miner to be a call-centre operator. In addition, local people may not be prepared to work for the wages on offer for those jobs.

But the solution is not to throw the 1.5 million British unemployed on the scrap heap, and import millions of immigrants with low expectations. Retraining and work placement schemes have proved effective in making sure those out of work can do the jobs available. But employers will have little incentive to support such active labour market policies if it is simply cheaper and easier to bring in immigrants.

Likewise it is true that many unemployed don't want to work for the wages available, but companies can only get away with paying such low wages because there is always a willing supply of cheap immigrant labour to do it (see chapter 18).

In the meantime, unskilled British youth too often conclude that rather than work for such paltry wages, it is far more attractive to get involved in crime or deal drugs. The destruction of unskilled jobs and the importation of unskilled labour means that we have undermined unskilled workers in Britain to such an extent that it can seem a rational choice to stay out of the labour market and get involved in crime.

To take another example, there are no skills shortages in Britain when it comes to nursing—there are in fact 100,000 fully-trained nurses in Britain not working in nursing because the pay and conditions are so bad; on top of that one third of nurse trainees don't bother finishing their course because they become so disillusioned. And yet the NHS is importing tens of thousands of foreign nurses—not because there are skills shortages in the UK, but because it is easier and cheaper to recruit nurses from the world's poorest countries than it is to improve the pay and conditions of nurses in Britain.

Big business and the Confederation of British Industry often complain about labour shortages and use that to justify immigration. But businesses likes immigration for the same reason they like high unemployment—they want as big a pool of willing labour as possible because it makes it a buyer's market for them.

The contention that Europe or the UK have generalised labour shortages crumbles even further when you dig deeper and look at 'participation rates'—the proportion of those of working age actually in work or looking for it. Only one third of men work until the retirement age of 65—and many want to carry on working even beyond that but are forced out of the labour market by mandatory retirement policies. Lack of childcare facilities in the UK means that women here are far less likely to work than they are, for example, in Scandinavia. Overall, fewer men and women of working age are actually in work in the UK than other countries such as the USA, Denmark or Switzerland. According to a 1990 study, if the EU raised participation rates up to Danish levels, then it would add 30 million workers to the labour market. The Council of Europe's 2001 report *Europe's Population and Labour Market Beyond 2000* concluded Europe still suffers from the same problems as it did throughout the 1990s:

> Europe today suffers from very high levels of under-utilisation of its potential labour force, reflected both in high unemployment levels and low participation rates.

Looking to the future, the report concludes:

> Unemployment levels and continuing increases in productivity make it very unlikely that a general labour shortage will appear in Europe.

Furthermore, because of its language, Britain is also the main destination for many migrant workers from the EU. There are hundreds of thousands of young workers from Spain, Italy, France and Greece in the UK already, keen to improve their English, a massive addition to the labour supply—particularly unskilled labour—without recourse to non-EU immigration. This will obviously increase sharply when the EU enlarges to the East.

18

How immigration can lead to worse pay and conditions for native workers

Immigration is usually portrayed by the pro-immigration lobby as a free lunch for everyone. It is not. There are clear winners and losers, and any immigration policy has to be based on balancing out the interests of those winners and losers, and of the immigrants themselves.

The economics of this issue are well established and documented. In short, those who employ immigrants or have a skill set that complements them gain from immigrant labour; those who compete with immigrants lose. Companies that like cheap or compliant labour, and the middle classes that like cheap cleaners and waiters win; the unskilled who compete with unskilled immigrants lose.

Lord Richard Layard, director of the Centre for Economic Performance at the London School of Economics, one of the top labour economists in the country and designer of Labour's welfare-to-work programme, has been equally frustrated by the consensus that immigration is a free lunch, and wrote in a letter to the *Financial Times*:

> 'Europe needs immigrants, skilled and unskilled', you say. This may now be the conventional wisdom, but it glosses over the conflicts of interest between different groups of Europeans.
>
> For European employers and skilled workers, unskilled immigration brings real advantages. It provides labour for their restaurants, building sites and car parks and helps to keep these services cheap by keeping down the wages of those who work there.
>
> But for unskilled Europeans, it is a mixed blessing. It depresses their wages and may affect their job opportunities. Already unskilled workers are four times more likely to be unemployed than skilled workers, and it is not surprising that they worry.
>
> Although the total size of the labour force has no effect on the unemployment rate, its structure does; and a rise in the proportion of workers who are unskilled does raise overall unemployment. By the same token we do need more immigration of skilled workers, to rebalance our workforce.
>
> But the main argument for unskilled immigration is the interests of the immigrants, not those of 'Europe'. It is not helpful

to say that 'Europe needs unskilled immigration', as if all the Europeans were the same. We need to allow for the different interests at stake.

Obviously, the ability to employ the top Italian bankers, American managers and Indian IT specialists helps Britain's economy and creates wealth we all enjoy. But that is a small portion of the overall level of total migration to the UK, which amounted to almost half a million people in 2000. There is an immense amount of unskilled immigration, as well as skilled migrants ending up in unskilled jobs because of lack of language skills, knowledge of the labour market and so on.

Concerned about the economic and demographic impact of record levels of immigration, the US government commissioned the US National Academy of Sciences to assemble a panel of the country's top economists and demographers to compile a report on the subject. Published in 1997, *The New Americans: Economic, Demographic, and Fiscal Effects of Immigration* stated:

> Along with immigrants themselves, the gainers are the owners of productive factors that are complementary with the labor of immigrants—that is, domestic, higher-skilled workers, and perhaps owners of capital—whose incomes will rise. Those who buy goods and services produced by immigrant labor also benefit. The losers may be the less-skilled domestic workers who compete with immigrants and whose wages will fall. To the extent that immigrants specialize in activities that otherwise would not have existed domestically, immigration can be beneficial for all domestic residents.

The British Home office seems to have accepted these conclusions. Its study *Migration: an economic and social analysis* says:

> In general, migration increases the supply of labour: this is likely, in theory, to reduce wages for workers competing with migrants, and increase returns to capital and other factors complementary to migrant labour. In general, this redistribution will hurt workers who own factors of production which are complementary to migrants, and help those who own factors of production that are substitutes.

Because Britain already has a surplus of unskilled labour, then any increase in the unskilled labour pool simply makes their life more difficult. There has been much commentary on the creation of an alienated unskilled underclass—many of them from ethnic minorities—who have no stake in society because there are no jobs for them. However, the pro-immigration lobby—who usually claim they care about unskilled workers—are very keen to play down the impact. Although there appears to be no research on the UK situation, there has been a lot of research in the US. The National Academy of Sciences report concluded:

> Immigration over the 1980s increased the labor supply of all workers by about four percent. On the basis of evidence from the literature on labor demand, this increase could have reduced the wages of all competing native-born workers by about one or two per cent.

The decline of wages for unskilled workers has been one of the main challenges facing America, not just consigning many unskilled workers to poverty, but encouraging the growth of an alienated underclass, and increasing the inequality between the rich and poor. The evidence is that this is largely a result of unskilled immigration.

The NAS report found that although the general wage decline was one per cent or two per cent, it is the most vulnerable members of society who suffer most, particularly the poorly educated, and African-Americans who live in areas of high immigration. Its conclusion stated:

> Based on previous estimates of responses of wages to changes in supply, the supply increase due to immigration lowered the wages of high school dropouts by about five percent, that is, about 44 percent of the total decline in wages of high school dropouts observed between 1980 and 1994.

In 1995, the US government's Bureau of Labour Statistics published research estimating that a full 50 per cent of real wage loss among low-skilled Americans is due to competition from low-skilled immigrants.

The US Centre for Immigration Studies in a 1998 report suggested that for the 25 million Americans employed in low-skilled jobs, their wages were reduced by 12 per cent or $1,915 per person as a result of the influx of unskilled workers. It found that a one per cent increase in immigrants leads to a 0.8 per cent decrease in unskilled wages, and that those who suffer worst are minorities--blacks and Hispanics.

Robert Reich, the Harvard economics professor and President Clinton's labour secretary, said: 'Undoubtedly, access to lower-wage foreign workers has a depressing effect on wages.'

A 1994 study in Germany found similar effects from the impact of Turkish immigration: it depressed the wages of blue-collar workers, and increased that of white-collar workers. One of the NAS report's authors, George Borjas, professor of public policy at Harvard University, and a Cuban émigré himself, wrote in a 1996 an article for *Atlantic Monthly* entitled 'The New Economics of Immigration': 'I have estimated that native workers lose about $133 billion a year as a result of this immigration (or 1.9 percent of the gross domestic product in a $7 trillion economy), mainly because immigrants drive down wages.'

After the pro-immigration lobby and government widely promoted the NAS report as saying that immigration benefits every US citizen, Professor Borjas was moved to co-author an article in the *New York Times*:

> We have been distressed to hear public officials repeatedly misrepresent [the NAS study's] findings as the immigration debate has evolved in the last seven months ... these officials make it seem as if immigration is a free lunch for Americans... Low-income workers and taxpayers in immigrant states lose; those who employ immigrants or use immigrant services win, as do the immigrants themselves. The critical issue is how much we care about the well-being of immigrants compared with that of the Americans who win and the Americans who lose.

As well as these econometric measurements there is endless anecdotal evidence of the way that immigration undercuts native workers. In the San Diego tomato industry, workers were paid $4 an hour in the 1980s, until crews of illegal aliens allowed the employers to reduce the wage to $3.35. All the veterans unwilling to work for that wage were forced to leave the fields. The unionised furniture factories of San Francisco were undercut and forced out of business by the lower-paying immigrant-laden plants of Southern California. In the Mission Foods tortilla factory strike, management lowered wages by 40 per cent and when native workers went on strike, they simply replaced them with Mexican immigrants. A 1998 General Accounting Office study found that a decade of heavy immigration to Los Angeles had changed the janitor industry from a mostly unionised higher paid black workforce to a non-unionised lower paid Hispanic one. During the period of 1925 to 1965, when there was virtually no immigration to the US, the economy not only powered ahead, but the pay and conditions of African-Americans was raised sharply as their labour became more in demand. They have since been undercut by repeated waves of large-scale immigration.

A report from the RAND organisation by noted immigration scholars Kevin McCarthy and George Vernez said that in 1990 competition with immigrants for jobs caused between 128,200 and 194,000 workers in California to withdraw from the workforce. Most of those workers were minorities or women.

The arguments that the British pro-immigration lobby use to counter this don't stand up to scrutiny. Migrants, they say, fills jobs that otherwise wouldn't be done, and in so doing create other jobs for native workers. The classic example is in Germany, where Turkish workers did the work Germans didn't want to do, allowing native Germans to move up the work ladder and do management jobs. This effect is no doubt true, but importing an underclass to raise the status of natives is a rather one-off economic policy that cannot be sustained forever because of its implications for population growth, let alone social cohesion. It would require either insisting that the progeny of the underclass remain an underclass and don't try and better themselves, or it would require the perpetual importation of an underclass to raise the status of each new generation of native workers. Neither is desirable.

Often it is said that immigrants will do jobs that natives don't want to, or can't, do. Certainly, high levels of job vacancies can exist side by side with high levels of unemployment, as we can see in London which suffers levels of joblessness far above the national average. But the solution is to make the labour market work more effectively, retrain people and improve their incentives to work, rather than simply ignore the 1.5 million British unemployed and bring in cheap foreign labour.

Obviously a lot of people don't work in the UK because the wages they can get are so low—who wants to work for the minimum wage, which amounts to just £8,000 a year? The answer: immigrants who come from even poorer countries. The Home Office recognised this in its report *Migration: an Economic and Social Analysis*, adding that it could lead to higher native unemployment and lower GDP per capita:

> If native workers are not prepared to accept a wage below a given floor, and migration leads to the market wage for some native workers falling below that floor, then migration could in theory lead to an increase in native unemployment. While overall output will not fall, output per head and output attributable to natives may do so. Whether this happens in any particular case is of course an empirical question.

An empirical question, it has to be said, that the Home Office has made no attempt to answer. The best way of helping the unskilled in Britain is to ensure there are jobs that pay a living wage, but with record levels of immigration that is never going to happen.

Immigration means that McDonald's can get away with paying the minimum wage in one of the world's most expensive cities, that the NHS can get away with paying a pittance to nurses, that schools can get away with paying a pittance to teachers.

Even skilled people can suffer from immigration competition. Surgeons have resisted government attempts to bring in foreign surgeons, because it will reduce their private earnings. British IT contractors have complained bitterly about the government bringing in so many IT workers, even during recession, because it depresses their wages and leads to higher unemployment. The American Engineering Association fervently opposes issuing too many visas to foreign engineers. However, for skilled workers it is quite possible that, although their wages may suffer from immigration, the overall benefit to society is positive because it makes their services more widely available.

Reducing immigration, and so reducing the supply of labour, can only be good for those already in the labour market. The less competition there is, the more workers are empowered to improve their pay and conditions. Doctors, barristers and actors all restrict entry into their profession in the UK because ensuring shortages help them improve their pay and conditions. If labour shortages do arise as our society ages, they will force the pace of adjustments that we as a society inevitably have to make at some point (see chapter 15).

There will be nothing like modest labour shortages to encourage industry and society to genuinely embrace family-friendly working. If companies can't get the working parents on their own terms, they will have to make more effort to give working parents what they want, and that means embracing more flexible hours, crèches at work and so on. It will put pressure on a reluctant government to give tax breaks for childcare and better parental leave.

Similarly, it will force companies to stop being so ageist, end the culture of early retirement and instead train and retain older workers, treating them like the valuable human capital they are.

Large-scale immigration will merely discourage us from making the changes we will inevitably have to make at some point to adapt to an ageing society.

19

Why unskilled immigration is no saviour for failing industries and makes businesses less competitive

Indulging industry's addiction to cheap labour can also prevent it from improving its competitiveness in other ways, such as increasing mechanisation, adding value and improving quality. By discouraging them from improving competitiveness in more appropriate ways, importing cheap labour can encourage industries to adopt strategies that will ensure their eventual demise.

The textile factories of the Midlands and North of England paid so little that no native person wanted to work in them and so they imported thousands of workers from South Asia. But that just gave them a blood transfusion that kept them going for a few more years before they were inevitably forced to close, leaving the Asian communities languishing with high unemployment and poverty. The industry is long gone, but the towns are left with immense social and economic problems. If the industries had attempted to compete instead by improving their designs or mechanising, rather than paying lower wages, then there is a chance there might even now be something left of them.

Paul Barker of the Institute of Community Studies wrote in the London *Evening Standard* (17 May 2002):

> I was brought up just over the hills from Burnley, and it's true that in South Lancashire and West Yorkshire the short-term drafting-in of immigrants to keep clapped-out textile mills going—rather than spend money on new capital equipment—was a social disaster. Before long, the mills closed anyway. Thousands of Asians were dumped onto the unemployment register. So were thousands of whites. All were victims of an ill-thought-through policy.

We will never be able to compete with low-wages labour-intensive industries of developing nations (for the simple reason that our cost of living is higher), and it is a mistake to try. The factories of Northern Italy are going down exactly this route now—they say they cannot compete without offering wages so low no Italian wants to do them, and so must have large-scale immigration.

As David Coleman, professor of demography at Oxford University, told *The Times* (15 November 2001): 'reliance on the apparently easy option of importing (cheap) labour from overseas might not help Europe's central economic problem of low productivity'.

On a basic macro-economic level, the key to sustained economic growth per capita is raising labour productivity, and deliberate attempts to simply increase the supply of labour will act reduce labour productivity—or slow down the growth of labour productivity—thus harming the prospects for long-run per capita economic growth. In other words, relying on immigration could reduce GDP per capita (see chapter 21).

20

Creating co-dependency: the fallacy of arguing Britain would collapse without immigrants

It is often said in justification of immigration that Britain—and in particular London—would grind to a halt without immigrants, which is no doubt true. But this is a post-facto justification of immigration that has already happened, rather than an argument to justify immigration that is set to happen in the future.

Obviously, if you import a large pool of labour, and they start working, then a dependency is created between the native population and the immigrants. You could import a hundred million workers to the UK, and they will set to work, and after ten years the pro-immigration lobby will say that the economy would collapse without them, which would no doubt be true. It will also point out the amazing achievements that many of them will inevitably have made—and there will no doubt be amongst all the immigrants a large number of remarkable intellectuals, entrepreneurs and so on. But that doesn't mean you want to import a hundred million workers.

Such post-facto justifications fail to take into account what the scenario would have been in the absence of immigration. The alternative may well have been lower unemployment, the absence of an alienated and criminalised underclass, more family-friendly practices to get mothers back to work, and an abandonment of the ageist practice of throwing men in their fifties into premature retirement. If we had gone down that route, the anti-immigration lobby could then say: 'Thank God we didn't have large-scale immigration'. The idea that a mature, large nation like Britain has to have immigrants to survive is demonstrably fallacious. The restaurants of Rome are well served without immigrants; Norway ticks along nicely without immigrants.

21

Importing poverty: why immigration can make a country poorer and doesn't increase long-term economic growth

We are repeatedly told by the Chancellor Gordon Brown and others that immigration boosts economic growth. This is, as the Americans say, a no-brainer. It is also disingenuous. Immigration boosts population growth, and every extra person working will increase economic output. The only way immigration could fail to boost the economy is if no immigrants worked and brought no funds with them.

But the only measurement that matters is what effect immigration has on GDP per capita and what effect it has on long-term growth of GDP per capita. What matters to people is not how big the economy is, but how rich they are, and how quickly they are getting richer.

However, there is very little evidence that the present scale and type of the net immigration to UK has a positive impact on either, and lots of evidence that it makes us poorer as a country and reduces long-term growth. The US National Academy of Science's report summarises the issues like this:

> In the long run, assuming constant returns to scale, immigrants can affect rates of economic growth only to the extent that they differ from the native-born—if, for example, they arrive with a different mix of skills from those of native-born workers. To have an effect on growth rates, this difference between immigrants and natives must persist over each new generation. If the children of immigrants—or, if not the children, the grandchildren and great-grandchildren—come to be just like the native-born, then all that immigration does is augment the population and the scale of the economy; it does not change the rate of growth of income per capita.
>
> Overall, in the massive and complex US economy, immigration is unlikely to have a very large effect on relative earnings or on gross domestic product per capita. Among the legions of factors that affect the economy, many are far more critical than immigration, including savings and investment and the human capital of US workers.

The American economy has grown rapidly over the last quarter of a century because its population has grown rapidly, largely as a result of immigration; but GDP per capita has grown by a very unimpressive two per cent a year, almost identical to Europe's rate of growth with far less immigration. In contrast, between 1925 and 1965, the USA had virtually no immigration and became the world's strongest economy and one of its richest countries. Before the bursting of its asset bubble, Japan had sustained extremely high levels of growth for decades without any immigration. Norway has attained the highest quality of life in the world, according to the 2002 UN Human Development Report, in the almost total absence of immigration.

The Economic Council of Canada, in its 1991 study *The Economic and Social Impacts of Immigration*, found that economic growth per capita grew fastest when net immigration was zero or even negative. In its report 'Charting Canada's Future', the Canadian Department of Health and Welfare found that there was no correlation between population growth and economic growth in the 22 countries of the OECD. In 1985, the Macdonald Commission in Canada said that: 'The broad consensus ...is that high levels of immigration will increase aggregate variables such as labour force, investment and real gross income, but cause... real income and real wages to decline.'

There are two issues here—first the scale of the net immigration, averaging 180,000 a year to Britain between 1998 and 2000, which simply acts as a spur to population growth. Secondly, the actual type of immigration and the skills they bring (tackled further down).

Unfortunately for the pro-immigration lobby, the assumption made by the National Academy about constant returns to scale (or economies of scale) doesn't apply in the UK. In empty countries, such as Australia and Canada, which both have active immigration programmes, there are probably positive economies of scale in increasing the population density from very low levels, because it gives you the critical mass to afford roads and other infrastructure, particularly in remote areas.

But in a country as crowded as the UK there are significant diseconomies of scale on the national level. Congestion in London and the South East both on roads and public transport is a huge brake on growth. Attempts to control congestion—such as congestion charging in London, tight controls on parking, increasing fuel duties—also inevitably curb economic activity because they prevent businesses doing what they would otherwise want to.

Shortage of land on which to build factories, offices and retail centres, slows down business's expansion plans. Exorbitant property prices—the result of high population and land shortage—also puts brakes on all businesses from entrepreneurial start-ups to large corporations. Britain has a booming airline industry which is being held back by the difficulty in finding anywhere to put more runways. The government wants to build more incinerators, but can't find anywhere to put them. The battle between land use and business development got so extreme in Newbury that Vodafone ended up threatening to pull its headquarters out of the town unless it could build new head offices on one site.

Nor does increasing the population make everyone richer by increasing the size of the market. There will be some positive economies of scale but, in an open economy like Britain that has a large volume of imports and exports, the effects will be small.

The countries with the three largest populations in the world—China, India and Indonesia—are notable for their poverty, while many countries with tiny populations—such as Norway, Luxembourg, New Zealand, Iceland—are notable for their affluence and high quality of life. There is no evidence that simply having a large population makes people richer.

In short, there is no reason to believe that the simple act of expanding the UK's population from 60 million to 70 million will increase GDP per capita, and lots of reasons to believe it will reduce it. In other words, if all the net immigration of 180,000 a year had the same skill set and employability as the native population, their entrance into the UK would make most Britons worse off.

Since immigration doesn't boost GDP per capita by boosting population growth, it can only do so if immigrants bring with them a set of skills or capital investment that boosts growth. The pro-immigration lobby loves to quote Treasury estimates that immigrants are responsible for ten per cent of economic output, even though they only account of eight per cent of the population. Government figures show that immigrants suffer higher unemployment than the native born (six per cent compared to five per cent), but those that do work earn on average 12 per cent higher wages.

But such broad generalisations are disingenuous because they overlook the impact of different types of immigration. They lump together the army of professionals from North America, Europe and Japan working in highly paid specialised jobs, most notably in the City, with immigrants groups such as those from Bangladesh and Pakistan who suffer very high levels of unemployment. This is reflected in the income figures. While immigrants are twice as likely to earn over £50,000 a year as the native born (including figures such as the chief executive of Barclays, the manager of the England football team and Sir Magdi Yacoub), there are also far more immigrants who earn low wages.

By its very nature, those that come to the UK through the work permit programme have virtually nil unemployment and enjoy high wages, and most of these come from high-income countries with the single biggest nationality being the US (although an increasing number from Africa and India). Australians and New Zealanders coming to Britain with holiday working visas have high levels of education, low level of unemployment while here, and almost always return home.

Together with immigration from the EU, most of this is balanced migration, sharing skills between high-income countries, together with some low level net immigration of skilled professionals from low-income countries. British citizens go to work in North America and Europe, and North Americans and Europeans come to work in Britain. It is of high economic value, usually temporary and, because it is a balanced flow in both directions, doesn't contribute to the record net immigration of 183,000 people, sparking population growth etc.

As earlier figures showed, most migration between Britain and other high-income countries is balanced, and the net immigration of 183,000 to the UK is entirely from the Third World and Eastern Europe. Such immigration can be extremely beneficial—the one-off immigration of highly educated, skilled and economically successful Ugandan Asians has definitely made a major contribution to the UK economy.

But the current sustained high level of net immigration from low-income countries are people who, once here, demonstrably suffer higher unemployment and have lower incomes than the average population (and, in the case of most but not all ethnic minority communities, this relative poverty is also visited on the children of immigrants). It is difficult to see how that can do anything other than have a short-term downward impact on the GDP per capita. The Americans—who have 1.3 million immigrants a year, almost entirely from the Third World—have a term for it: 'importing poverty'.

The effects of importing poverty in New York City were clearly shown by the 2000 census, which revealed a puzzling drop in median income. The staunchly pro-immigration *New York Times* reported that the decline in incomes was 'traceable in large part to immigration, according to new census data that show income declines concentrated heavily in neighborhoods in the Bronx, Brooklyn and Queens that have become magnets for new arrivals'.

A study by the Public Policy Institute of California, *Trends in Family and Household Poverty*, directly related the rise in poverty in the state to the high level of Third World immigration. According to the report, poverty in California has risen in five of the six household types—married, no children; married with children; single parent with children; other family; non-family and live alone.

However, across the nation, poverty has declined in five of the six categories. Overall, California's poverty rates have increased much faster than other states and are 1.3 times higher than in the rest of the country, and this has nothing to do with any economic downturn. It said:

> long-term trends indicate that increases in poverty are more than temporal changes due to business cycles... the growing proportion of households headed by less-educated, often immigrant, adults explains much of the increase [in poverty].

A large part of net immigration to the UK is from Pakistan and Bangladesh—largely through marriage and family reunion—but the generally very isolated Pakistani and Bangladeshi communities suffer extreme poverty and rates of unemployment approaching 50 per cent. It is almost certain that this type of immigration depresses GDP per capita, not raises it.

What of the long-run effects? As the National Academy of Science report says, if the children or grandchildren of immigrants become just like the native born, then all that happens is the economy has a one-off increase in size, but the trend rate of growth remains the same and so there will be no long-run impact on GDP per capita.

Often differences do persist over generations, and can positively contribute to trend rates of growth. White immigration to South Africa (although it brought appalling social costs), Asian immigration to Kenya and Chinese immigration to Malaysia probably all pushed up the long-term growth rates above what they would otherwise have been.

It is often said that the UK benefits because immigrants are far more energetic and entrepreneurial than the native population, and certainly the business start-up rate is very high, and many, particularly Asians, have created large businesses employing many people (but see chapter 33).

However, poverty tends to persist in many immigrant groups in the UK, and trickles down the generations, although other immigrant groups have become wealthier. Poverty persists in the Pakistani and Bangladeshi communities, and Blacks of African and West Indian origin also have incomes below average. Incomes of Indian men and Chinese immigrants are much higher. I can find no evidence on children of white immigrants, but given the almost complete assimilation it would seem reasonable to assume they are on a par with the national average.

However, certainly for ethnic minorities, the average income per head remains below the national average, and unemployment remains twice the national average. It seems unlikely that the type of net immigration we have at the moment that leads to a growing sub-section of the population with below-average income and above-average unemployment will make any upward contribution to GDP per capita or the trend rate of growth.

As mentioned in chapter 19, relying on immigration to increase the labour pool and to supply cheap labour also reduces the incentive to increase labour productivity (why automate with a new machine when you can get cheap workers instead?). Increasing the labour pool rather than increasing labour productivity inevitably leads to a lower per capita productivity, which is the single most important way that a country generates wealth and raises the standard of living.

I leave the last word with Professor George Borjas, the most respected immigration economist in the US, and author of *Heaven's Door*, a book on the economic impact of immigration, which he concluded was insignificant (and that is before tax subsidies from the native-born to immigrants in the US are taken into account). His book met with mixed reviews, but he wrote in the foreword to the paperback edition that the most convincing argument was that no one had proved any more significant economic gains:

> Some reviewers also claimed that it was 'absurd' to conclude, as I do, that the net economic benefits from immigration are small, probably less than $10 billion a year. This estimate comes from a simple application of the widely used textbook model of a competitive labor market. This is the same model that is typically used to analyze the economic consequences of such government policies as minimum wages and payroll taxes. The market for ideas provides what is perhaps the most convincing argument in favor of my estimate. The immigration area, after all, is highly contentious. If it were that simple to show that the gains from immigration are huge, there is an audience ready and willing to buy such numbers. My estimates are so 'absurd' that not a single academic study has

concluded that they are higher—and some studies have concluded that they are lower.

This argument also applies to the UK. If there were real evidence of great economic gain, we would know about it.

22

How immigration increases inequality by making the rich richer and the poor poorer

Immigration such as we have in Britain increases the size of the economy, but not GDP per capita nor the long term growth rate. But by far the main economic effect is to transfer wealth from those who lose from immigration to those who win from it. Usually, but not always, this basically means the poor giving money to the rich.

George Borjas, professor of public policy at Harvard and probably the most respected US expert on the economics of immigration, wrote in *Atlantic Monthly* in 1996:

> The size of the economic pie increases. And a redistribution of income is induced, from native workers who compete with immigrant labor to those who use immigrants' services.

Put simply, in the UK, the members of the Confederation of British Industry win, and the members of the Trades Union Congress lose. Hospitals win, nurses lose.

The situation is actually somewhat more complex than Borjas states, because there are also some immigrants—particularly successful entrepreneurs—who employ natives and so increase their incomes.

Borjas estimates that, for the US, the 20 million foreign-born residents (including himself) cost native workers about $133 billion a year in lost wages. However, he estimates that employers—from the owners of large agricultural enterprises to people who hire household help—gain in the order of $140 billion, implying a net gain of about $7 billion, a minimal amount for a country the size of the US, and this is massively outweighed by the costs to taxpayers of increased costs of welfare, schools and hospitals. Borjas concludes:

> The debate over immigration policy is not a debate over whether the entire country is made better off by immigration—the gains from immigration seem much too small, and could even be outweighed by the costs of providing increased social services. Immigration changes how the economic pie is sliced up—and this

> fact goes a long way toward explaining why the debate over how many and what kinds of immigrants to admit is best viewed as a tug-of-war between those who gain from immigration and those who lose from it.

Immigrants to the US have lower levels of education and skills than the native population, and the effect of the immigration is to redistribute wealth from people on low incomes to people already on high incomes. The US Council of Economic Advisers said in 1994:

> Immigration has increased the relative supply of less educated labor and appears to have contributed to the increasing inequality of income.

Academic studies have suggested that the reason that income inequality has risen much faster in California than the rest of the US is because it has had so much more relatively unskilled immigration.

Obviously making heart surgeons—who are among the best paid professionals in the UK when you take into account private income—compete with immigrants will actually help reduce inequality in the UK. It will reduce their incomes (which is why they are resisting it), and reduce the bills of those who need the operations, who are usually far poorer than them.

However, very few immigrants from low-income countries, who are responsible for the entire net immigration to the UK, compete at the top end of the income scale, but further down (this is not generally true of immigrants who come from the developed world, including European, American and Japanese executives and bankers, but they largely just match skilled British emigrants leaving the UK).

The record number of immigrants from the developing world suffer lower incomes than natives, and they suffer higher levels of unemployment. Obviously, when it comes to ethnic minority immigrants these inequalities have so far been continued among their children and grandchildren. Thus the non-EU immigration of the current sort Britain is experiencing almost certainly contributes to the rising inequality Britain is seeing between rich and poor.

The contrast is Canada, which has an active immigration programme, but is very particular to ensure it only gets highly skilled and highly educated people. In contrast to the US, which has relied on unskilled immigration, Canada remains a far more equal society, with a far more limited alienated underclass.

23

Why free movement of labour is different from free movement of goods and capital

It is often said that immigration—free movement of labour—is merely an extension of the well-accepted benefits of free movement of goods (trade) and free movement of capital (international investment).

In one sense, this is certainly true. Allowing people to move from where their productivity is low to where their productivity is higher will raise the global output. It does this through increasing the livelihoods of immigrants themselves, and creating global centres of excellence such as the City of London, Hollywood and Silicon Valley.

However, this free-market argument, taken to its logical extension, implies the removal of all border controls, allowing a massive movement of people from low productivity areas to high productivity ones and so boosting the overall global economy.

The fact that so few people, including free market economists, support the removal of all border controls around the world, reflect the fact that there are significant drawbacks to this argument.

Firstly, it does nothing to raise productivity or promote economic development in poor countries, who will see the exodus of their most energetic and educated to the West (see chapter 34). In this way, it will promote a far more unbalanced world with all significant economic activity taking place in already industrialised countries, and the Third World condemned to perpetual poverty.

Secondly, there is a large difference between the movement of goods and capital and the movement of people, which has many more economic downsides.

Unlike people, goods and investment don't turn up uninvited, don't have legal rights, don't bring family members with them, don't use health services, consume welfare, lead to overcrowding, social tensions and race riots.

Most importantly, and this is the critical difference that marks a market failure in the free-market arguments, people cannot be sent back or thrown away when they are no longer needed.

It is a market failure because businesses that import labour profit from it when they need it, but society generally pays for the costs when they are no longer needed by the employer and become unemployed. If employers had to pay for the full cost of importing a worker—including paying their unemployment benefit, health and education costs when they were no longer employed—it is likely that they would import far fewer.

There are other examples of market failure in the movement of people which don't occur in the movement of goods and capital. Immigration is far less flexible than trade and international investment, in that it is usually a one-way process incapable of reflecting local labour market conditions—it is usually a permanent response to a temporary condition. Although highly skilled workers, and intra-company transfers tend to be highly mobile following the work, less skilled workers aren't because the significant costs involved in immigration are large hurdles for them. The British textile industry imported many thousands of textile workers from South Asia to help boost their productivity, but when they inevitably failed they left their work-forces in Britain destitute, with native taxpayers to pick up the tab.

Countries with very high tax-payer funded education systems (such as Canada) lose out to those without (such as the US) because immigrants get their education paid for by taxpayers in their country of origin, and then reap the rewards for it in a country where they pay lower taxes because they aren't paying for the education of others. On a global scale, this would undermine free university education in those countries that supply it.

Less productive immigrants have an incentive to move from countries without welfare systems to those with. The celebrated free-market economist Milton Friedman has said that having open borders is incompatible with having welfare systems. Similarly with health care—the UK experiences health migration by people seeking access to the free services of the NHS without having paid towards them, which on a large enough scale would totally undermine the NHS.

The free movement of goods and capital is in many ways a substitute for the free movement of people, making it unnecessary. Instead of moving workers from Asia to Britain, the British textile industry could have concentrated its efforts to move production to Asia (which happened anyway). Car makers from West Germany don't need to bring workers over from Eastern Europe because they can set up factories in Eastern Europe. This helps the car makers and consumers of the West, while helping the development of the economies of the East. This in the long run will do more for overall economic growth than creating displaced populations of migrant workers from Eastern Europe in the West.

In general, people like to live in communities where they grew up and relate to people, and to this extent the more that free movement of goods and capital makes movement of people unnecessary, the better for global human welfare.

The importation of the labour from low-productivity countries to high-productivity ones will also have a negative impact on the pay and conditions on those in high-productivity countries (see chapter 18). While there may be reasons to redistribute their wealth to workers from poor countries, we do usually pretend that in democratic countries people have the right to determine the policies that affect their lives. Moving 200 million Chinese people to Europe would almost certainly boost global economic output in the short to medium term, but Europeans have a right to say no to them, irrespective of global economic arguments.

24

How immigration from the Third World almost certainly increases taxes

There is a big debate about whether immigrants 'pay their way'—whether they consume more public services than they contribute in taxes. This matters politically because it determines whether native people pay more or less out of their pockets in tax because of immigration.

It is fair to say that there is concern on the racist right that immigrants are 'scroungers', coming to Britain to live off benefits and council housing and contributing little in taxes. But the level of British benefits are so low that there is little evidence that people are crossing the world simply to access them. It seems very unlikely that asylum seekers are paying people traffickers up to £5,000 and risking their lives getting into the UK simply to get benefits of around £50 a week.

However, the Home Office felt sufficiently worried by these concerns to produce a study *The Migrant Population in the UK: Fiscal Effects*. This report has been very widely quoted because it produced the only answer that is politically acceptable: the 8.4 per cent of the British population not born in Britain contribute £2.5 billion more in taxes than they consume in public goods, the equivalent of a reduction in income taxes of one penny in the pound.

However, the headline conclusion masks uncomfortable evidence about the fiscal impacts of different types of immigrants. In summary, the Home Office report finds that the only reason that the overall fiscal contribution is positive is because certain high-income, high-employment groups more than pay their way, and make up for the fact that other lower-income, low-employment groups that consume high levels of benefits don't pay their way.

Immigrants from the developed world, who are more likely to come through the work permit programme, have higher levels of education, higher employment and are less likely to claim benefits, and so more than pay their way.

Immigrants from the developing world, who are more likely to come through family reunion or asylum, are less likely to be employed, more likely to have no qualifications and more likely to consume high levels of benefits, and so are subsidised by UK taxpayers. In other words, immigrants from the developed world (who are more likely to return home) more than pay their way, whereas immigrants from the Third World (who are responsible for the entire record net immigration to the UK) do not on average pay their way.

This reflects studies in the US that show that the fiscal contribution (or cost) of an immigrant is positively correlated to the level of development of the migrants' country of origin.

The far more extensive government research from the US also suggests that many groups of immigrants don't pay their way and are subsidised by native taxpayers—for example, the average Mexican immigrant to the US consumes $55,000 more in government services and welfare than they contribute in taxes throughout their lifetime; an immigrant with no qualifications is subsidised to the tune of $89,000 through their lifetime. Those immigrants to the UK which have similar employment and welfare consumption patterns as Mexican immigrants to the US are similarly likely to be massively subsidised by the British taxpayer (although the overall pattern of immigration to the US is less skilled on average than that to the UK, and so total national comparisons should be treated with caution even if there are similarities between subgroups of immigrants).

First, it should be noted that the headline figure of £2.5bn is both highly uncertain, and constitutes a fraction of one per cent of the total UK economy, which has an output of £1,000 billion a year. The Home Office report actually says that immigrants contribute £31.2bn in taxes, and receive £28.8bn in benefits and services, and that these figures are subject to wide margins of error. If each is only out by five per cent in the opposite direction, immigrants overall would be a net drain on the taxpayer. The only honest conclusion is that the impact on the Treasury's coffers is insignificant.

Similar studies in the US and Sweden have suggested that their immigrants don't pay their way, while studies in Spain and Germany have suggested their immigrants do. In Sweden, the government estimates that the foreign born are 12.3 per cent of the population, and high unemployment and low incomes means that the net fiscal cost is 0.9 per cent of GDP.

The Home Office report makes many assumptions that are certain to downplay the cost of immigration. It makes no attempt to measure the special language needs of immigrant children, or the special health needs of many immigrants (which would be highest among those from the developing world). It ignores the fact that immigrants live disproportionately in the South East, where housing costs and so housing benefits are highest. The study was made for the year 2000 when Britain had enjoyed a sustained boom, one time when there should be a net contribution (overall, there was a budget surplus, so people in Britain as a whole paid more in taxes than they consumed in government services and welfare). The Home Office report minimises overall 'lifecycle' costs, since it doesn't take into account that immigrants are disproportionately of working age, and have yet to claim retirement benefits and medical costs of old age, and so are at the time of their lives when they certainly should be major net contributors.

The study lumps all immigrants in together, including bankers and industrialists from North America, the EU and Japan, professionals and holiday workers from the EU and Australia, students from everywhere, IT specialists from India, nurses from the Philippines, husbands and wives who come through arranged marriages from Bangladesh, India and Pakistan, parents and grandparents who are brought over by their descendants, and refugees.

These groups are certain to have very different rates of tax contribution and consumption of services, based on how high their unemployment is, what they earn and what their use of benefits and government services such as health care and education is.

The report's authors, who clearly feel somewhat uncomfortable with their headline conclusion, are as honest as they can be:

> While the annual fiscal impact is positive in aggregate, the migrant population is so heterogenous that it is almost certain to be negative for specific groups, defined by particular socio-economic characteristics.

The report says absolutely nothing about which groups these might be. It merely wonders about what can be done about this:

> The disparity in performance raises the question as to whether it is possible to predict and select migrants who are likely to generate positive net fiscal impacts by reference to a set of ostensible social and economic characteristics.

It raises the question, but doesn't answer it. The report then concludes that you shouldn't have to justify immigration on economic grounds, a curious conclusion for a report that aims to do just that:

> Although the fiscal impact is positive overall for the migrant population, it is likely that this aggregate result masks the differential performance of subsections of the population. However, the aims of the government are wider than the purely economic, and there may be some entirely legitimate government policies related to immigration and asylum which do not necessarily produce a positive fiscal impact—where the aims may be, for instance, humanitarian.

So who are the groups that are likely to have 'negative fiscal impacts'? Although the report doesn't venture to answer, it is clear from their source data who these groups are likely to be, and it goes through all the reasoning, but without reaching the conclusion.

First it states that the fiscal contribution is clearly going to be bigger for those doing better in the labour market:

> The association between fiscal impact, employment and income is more certain. Potential fiscal contribution clearly increases with the likelihood of full-time employment and income earned.

The report says that economic outcomes of immigration are closely related to the method of entry, with those coming through the work permit scheme having greater economic success than those coming through marriage and family reunion (which is the biggest single category of immigration). Overall, those immigrants who do work earn 12 per cent higher incomes than the native born, but that masks two extremes of high earners—who tend to come through the work permit scheme—and low earners who tend to come through other methods, such as asylum and family reunion. The fact is that most North American immigrants enter the UK through work permits, and immigration for family reunion is dominated by India, Pakistan and Bangladesh, with Africa rising fast in this category.

> Most North Americans and Canadian enter the UK with work permits, the category for spouses and fiancées is dominated by those from the Indian subcontinent.

Unemployment among immigrants in the UK is far less than it is among immigrants elsewhere in Europe, but still about a fifth more than the native born. Again it masks big differences between those from rich countries and those from poor ones.

The Home Office report shows that migrants from the US, Australasia and the European Union have the highest probability of being employed; those from Eastern Europe, the Indian subcontinent have higher unemployment and lower employment; people from the Middle East have the highest unemployment of all. Unemployment among Bangladeshi and Pakistani immigrants is at startlingly high levels among women. Only seven per cent of all Bangladeshi women, including those born in the UK, are in employment, compared to 15 per cent of Pakistani women, 54 per cent of Indian women, and 66 per cent of Caribbean and 64 per
hite women (according to the Cabinet Office's
roving Labour Market Achievements for Ethnic
n British Society).

Office study doesn't give the breakdown of
g benefits by nationality, but it does say that

immigrants on average claim more unemployment benefit, more housing benefit, more council tax benefit and more child benefit, but less disability benefit and less state pension than the native born. It is a fair assumption that those who have highest unemployment (namely those from Eastern Europe, Indian subcontinent and the Middle East) are most likely to claim benefits.

The study is clear that immigrants with higher educational achievement are more likely to pay their way:

> Migrants with higher educational qualifications have a higher probability of being employed and are less likely to claim state benefits.

Again, it is generally immigrants from the developed world who have the highest educational achievements (partly because they are more likely to come through the work permit scheme than family reunion). The study suggests that about 40 per cent of immigrants from the Indian subcontinent have no educational qualifications at all, and about 25 per cent of those from the Caribbean. In contrast, only around five per cent of immigrants from the US, Canada and Australasia and ten per cent of immigrants from the EU have no educational qualifications. Overall, 70 per cent of people with degrees are likely to be employed, whereas for those with no qualifications, only about 30 per cent. Immigrants from the Middle East are the exception to this rule, since they have high levels of education but still have high levels of unemployment (which suggests more should be done to help them find appropriate uses for their skills).

The Home Office doesn't break down the fiscal impact by type of immigrant, but it does say:

> Although it is likely that the positive fiscal impact of migrants to the UK is in part attributable to migrant's favourable age structure, it is largely a product of the high performance of certain sectors of the migrant population, which account for an average level of income above that of UK-born residents.

Although the UK government goes through all the reasoning that Third World immigrants don't pay their way and flinches from reaching the conclusion, the US government has no such qualms. The National Academy of Sciences report, commissioned by the US government, concluded that overall immigrants to the US cost each American household between $166 and $226 in taxes each year. But this masked the pattern, borne out by earlier studies, that immigrants from rich countries pay their way, those from poor countries don't:

> Across the immigrant population, the size of the net fiscal burden imposed on native residents varies significantly. It is by far the heaviest for households of immigrants originating in Latin America. Immigrants from Europe and Canada actually make an average net fiscal contribution. These differences arise because households of Latin American immigrants tend to have lower incomes and to include more school-age children than do other immigrant households.

Overall, the National Academy of Sciences concluded that 'each immigrant with less than a high school education will cost American taxpayers $89,000'. The average adult Mexican immigrant will consume throughout their life time $55,200 more in services than they contribute in taxes. In places where Mexican immigration is highest, native American households have to pay out more to support them. Households in California have to pay on average $1,178 more in taxes to pay towards Mexican immigrants. Given that the welfare state in Britain is far more generous than in the US, it is likely the subsidies required by immigrants from the Third World are higher here.

25

Chain migration: the problem of self-perpetuating migration

Chain migration is a well established phenomenon, recognised by the Home Office, which means that migration flows can become self-perpetuating. With loose immigration controls, letting one person immigrate may in fact mean that you end up letting in five people or more. The power of chain migration has serious and far-reaching implications for migration policy, which can be politically uncomfortable.

The Home Office Paper *Migration: an Economic and Social Analysis* (2001) puts it like this:

> While there may be some decline from the unusually high net migration levels of the last few years, the long-term trend is likely to be increasing for at least the medium term. Moreover, we know that higher migration flows are likely to be persistent (that is, the relatively high current levels of migration will in turn lead to higher levels of migration in the future than would otherwise have occurred): both because migrants acquire legal rights around family reunion, and because of chain migration effects (for example, through the spread of information about how to get to a particular destination country, the entry requirements, and how to find accommodation and work, and through the creation of a network of contacts and support in the destination country).

Chain migration happens for a wide variety of reasons. Once people have moved to the UK, they are allowed to bring a certain number of people with them. Under current UK rules, you can bring a fiancée or fiancé, a spouse, children, parents, grandparents, and even a long-term boyfriend or girlfriend—but only if the relationship is homosexual or they are still married to someone else. You are allowed to bring in unlimited numbers of husbands or wives, so long as you divorce the earlier ones you brought in. Obviously, there are large incentives to bring over parents or grandparents because they will receive free medical care on the NHS for the rest of their lives, which they may not do at home.

The scale of this family reunion is very large in the UK—in fact it is the largest class of immigration, particularly for immigrants from South Asia and Africa.

The UK is less generous than some countries have been in the past, with Italy, for example, at one time allowing people to bring in brothers, sisters and cousins, which means that once someone from a particular community has been allowed to stay, the potential for chain migration is almost unlimited. The person can bring in their siblings and cousins, they can bring their spouses, they in turn can bring their siblings and parents and so on *ad infinitum*.

However, at the start of the twenty-first century, the UK is among the most generous western countries. Canada, which has a major immigration programme but is very picky about whom it accepts, makes it very difficult even to bring over husband and wives unless you can prove that you can support them for at least ten years. The US requires a minimum income to bring over a spouse as evidence that you can support them. In 2002, both Denmark and Holland have placed strong controls on those who wish to bring over spouses.

Chain migration also happens because people encourage and facilitate more distant family and friends to join them, even if they don't have a legal right to bring them over. The friends and family learn about the different routes they can get to the UK, and they know they have someone to help when they get here. Asylum seekers have frequently told researchers that they choose the UK as a destination because they already know someone here, and that there are established communities here. People come to visit their friends or relatives in Britain, and then overstay, or else learn about how to stay here permanently.

Chain migration also results in and is caused by substantial 'category switching', whereby people use whatever legal means they can to stay. Visitors get temporary work visas or student visas, or get permission to stay here on compassionate grounds if they are suffering from illnesses such as

HIV; students get temporary work visas; people with temporary work visas get permanent work visas and the right to settle; after five years they can become full UK citizens. Britain is far more generous with granting citizenship to people who have only been here a relatively short time than many other European countries.

Chain migration builds up momentum because the routes of entry become established and part of an industrialised business. The rising level of immigration to the UK has resulted in an enormous industry of immigration lawyers and support groups that make it far easier for people to come to the UK. They are the legal end of a spectrum that at the criminal end has people-traffickers, who arrange the entire trip from beginning to end for people to enter the UK illegally. Both immigration lawyers and people traffickers, like all businesses, are keen to perpetually expand their customer base.

In a more indirect way, chain migration also occurs because ethnic lobby groups campaign to make it easier to bring more of their compatriots over. The most blatant example is the Irish in the US, who were successful in getting the US government to give preferential treatment to the Irish by giving Irish nationals a guaranteed number of green cards each year. Likewise, immigrant groups in the UK successfully campaigned to get the Labour government to drop the 'primary purpose rule' soon after it was elected in 1997, which meant that potential immigrants no longer had to show that they weren't marrying a British citizen simply to move to Britain. Arranged marriages solely for the purpose of immigration were instantly legitimised as a method of entry to the UK.

Large-scale chain migration also makes it increasingly politically difficult for a government to clamp down on it, because there will be extremely determined opposition from immigration lobby groups. It can mean that immigration policy is in effect taken out of the control of government, and handed to immigrant communities. This is seen in the US, where successive Democrat and Republican governments have done nothing to tackle the substantial illegal immigration from Mexico, despite widespread frustration from most Americans, because they are worried about losing the increasingly large Hispanic vote. In Britain, the Conservative Party, which is by instinct immigration restrictionist, has banned its politicians from talking about immigration because it may lose votes from immigrants.

The scale and power of chain migration should not be underestimated. It means that even when Britain in theory had a policy of zero immigration, in reality immigration was running at historically unprecedented levels of nearly 200,000 people a year. It also means that a country loses control of who it lets in and who it doesn't, with new immigrants being chosen by more recent immigrants rather than by the government or people at large (this is why Canada is so tough on the causes of chain migration).

Large-scale chain migration also leads to social fragmentation because it means that communities of one nationality who already know each other from their home country can establish themselves very rapidly, and have little incentive to integrate or indeed interact with the host community. Large-scale chain migration, as we have in the UK, is a very effective way to ensure that immigrant communities become and remain socially and economically isolated.

British government ministers have said that the very strong preference for British Bangladeshis and Pakistanis to marry people from their 'home' country, who often don't speak English and have little knowledge of Britain, and bring them back to the UK, is largely responsible for the isolation and poor economic achievement of those communities. The former head of the Commission for Racial Equality, Gurbux Singh, said in 2002 that he could understand why Bangladeshis wanted to create 'little Bengal' in Britain, but didn't think they should try.

Because the consequences of it are so large, chain migration must be considered in any reform of the immigration system. Once chain migration has become well established, it means that the only way to reduce immigration is to tackle the causes of chain migration—such as making it far more difficult to bring relatives and partners over, more difficult to get permanent residence and so on.

It also means that if you have not taken tough measures to firmly control chain migration, then if you want to maintain control over future immigration, it becomes rational to give preference to those immigrants from groups that don't spark large-scale chain migration.

For example, there is a large difference between giving work permits to Japanese or South Koreans (who have small families and come from a rich country, are unlikely to get involved in much chain migration because they have no incentive to and are in any case likely to want to go back to Japan or South Korea), and giving work permits to Indians or Nigerians (who because they on average have larger families and come from a poor countries, are far more likely to stay in the UK and promote strong chain migration effects).

In short, easing up immigration controls on countries that have exhibited virtually no chain migration effects is unlikely to result in large unbalanced flows of populations in the future one way or another. The very limited chain migration effects from other EU countries in the last decade of the twentieth century meant that it was possible to open the borders within the EU without resulting in destabilising movements of population.

However, with countries that have shown strong chain migration effects, the opposite is likely to be true. That is why the Labour government's determination to swing the balance of holiday worker visas from Australians to Africans is not the apparently neutral act that it appears. Australians are far more likely to return to Australia, and far less likely to get involved in chain migration processes, so giving holiday working visas to Australians does not establish a growing and unbalanced flow of population (although large-scale, the flow of population is stable and balanced with virtually equal numbers coming and going). In contrast, giving holiday working visas to Zimbabweans is far more likely to result in encouraging large-scale net immigration from Zimbabwe over the longer term, through virtually all the different processes of chain migration.

Taking into account the effects of chain migration means that it may well be rational to seek policies which further mutually reduce immigration restrictions with countries such as Japan, South Korea, Australia or Canada, but not for other countries as Zimbabwe or Russia.

26

The drawbacks of multi-cultural societies

There has in public life been a sustained dialogue extolling the benefits of a multi-racial—and in particular multi-cultural—society. From politics to newspapers to TV programmes and book awards, few opportunities have been missed to celebrate multi-cultural Britain. No novel as far as I am aware has been publicly lauded as a denouncement of multi-cultural Britain.

The imperative to publicly celebrate multi-cultural Britain is obviously a reaction to the fact that actually there is widespread public unease with the whole notion. The public celebration of multi-cultural society is necessary to fight racism and xenophobia, and to make sure that ethnic minorities feel at home in the land of their birth. These are extremely laudable reasons to celebrate multi-cultural Britain, but not necessarily honest ones.

There are indeed many benefits of a multi-cultural society. It is undoubtedly culturally enriching, stimulating innovative music, film and literature. It is one of the glories of multi-culturalism that London contains both Westminster Abbey and the Neasden Temple, the largest Hindu temple outside India. While Christian churches are dying, Hindus put up one of the most beautiful places of worship in the country. The multi-racial society is also a far more exciting place to live, and as is often said, multi-racialism ensures a far better range of foods and restaurants.

But any honest assessment must acknowledge rather than suppress the fact there are also real drawbacks to a multi-racial society. An honest assessment is particularly important for countries such as Denmark, which is almost totally white but has been edging against the wishes of its population towards multi-culturalism. While ethnic minority communities are building in some areas of Copenhagen, the Danish are asking themselves whether they really want to encourage going down that multi-cultural route or discourage it. Similarly, the British government has embarked on policies that ensure that Britain will become far more multi-cultural than it is already, and it is reasonable for the population to ask if that is in their interest. An honest—rather than politically correct—assessment of multi-culturalism is the only way to do that. The celebration of multi-culturalism, though done for the best of reasons, cannot be left unexamined if it steps over from making immigrants welcome to promoting mass-immigration to the UK.

The most obvious drawback is that it leads to a society that is clearly ill at ease with itself, and becomes obsessed with the corrosive issue of racism. Race riots, which in the grand scheme of things are relatively rare, are merely the public violent outburst of tensions that are there much of the time. There is ongoing and sustained racial violence, which, as figures from the Commission for Racial Equality show, works both ways: black on white as well as white on black (although blacks are obviously far more likely to be victims).

There is tension between whole communities, which leads to ghettoisation and social divisions, as we have seen in many Northern towns. This is not so much cultural enrichment, as large-scale alienation of communities. In some small parts of the country one monoculture has replaced another to such an extent that it is possible to wander around some parts of Northern towns and not see white faces for hours.

The spectre of racism obviously pervades not just where people live, but where they work, damaging both those who suffer from prejudice and whole organisations. The convulsions that the Metropolitan Police are going through over the issue of institutional racism are obviously a consequence of being a multi-racial society—it simply wouldn't be relevant in a mono-racial one. The unease over multi-racialism has ended up with the government imposing quotas on all public bodies—the police, schools and even the Home Office's immigration services—to recruit a certain proportion of staff from ethnic minorities. That extraordinary level of interference—which requires substantial amount of management time in enactment, monitoring and so on—simply isn't necessary in a mono-racial society.

It can also lead to a remarkable degree of racial paranoia in the host community. One very politically correct publisher determined to celebrate multi-racialism told me with dismay about their experience with a black man who applied for a job. They went painstakingly through all the appropriate equal opportunities procedures, but he just wasn't the best candidate, and wasn't offered the post. He sued them for racial discrimination, and rather than have the public embarrassment of an organisation worried about its public image defending an accusation of racism in an industrial tribunal, they simply paid him £10,000—an act that obviously richly rewards and encourages such behaviour.

The race commentator Yasmin Alibhai-Brown wrote about this phenomenon in the *Evening Standard* on 24th June 2002, saying that a blanket accusation of racism against white people...

> ...encourages some black and Asian people to believe that everything that happens to them is because of white racism or (even worse) it enables the knaves among them to use racism as a poison to destabilise and terrorise organisations. Some of the guilty black workers involved in the Victoria Climbie case, where a young African child was tortured to death by black foster parents, did exactly that. There are already too many black activists who knowingly using these tactics. And, since the Lawrence enquiry, organisations are very easily unnerved. You only have to observe the fearful atmosphere in the Law Society since their deputy ex-chair, Kamlesh Bahl, part-won her case against it for discrimination to see what I mean.

Obviously, largely mono-cultural societies such as Denmark that are being turned against the wishes of the majority of their people into multi-cultural ones can only look at such national neuroses with trepidation.

There is also the issue of crime. It has been established beyond academic doubt that young black men are far more likely to commit violent street crimes including muggings than young white men. Only in 2002 did this become an issue that black leaders started publicly talking about, with the editor of the *Voice* newspaper breaking the silence and insisting that the black community must no longer duck this issue of alienation and criminality among young black men.

The Metropolitan Police estimate that black men are responsible for 63 per cent of muggings in the capital—in other words, their presence almost triples the rate of muggings (*Evening Standard*, 11 October 2002). After a 2002 Home Office study which concluded that young black men were primarily responsible for the increase in mobile phone crime, the most senior ethnic minority policeman, Metropolitan Police Assistant Commissioner Tarique Ghaffur, said in an interview with the *Daily Mail*:

> Research shows that most of these youngsters involved in this sort of criminal career progression are from black and other minority communities and this has implications for the long-term harmony of race relations in the UK. The minority communities in London, and elsewhere, must now accept more responsibility for the development of their own communities, and the trends in youth offending and social disintegration of all kinds.

Increasing immigration from parts of the world with high prevalence of disease and poor health services can also impact on public health in Britain. The government's Public Health Laboratory Service is quite clear that the rise in tuberculosis to the highest level in decades is because of increased immigration from countries with a high prevalence of TB. Similarly, the escalation of HIV to record levels in the UK is because of large-scale immigration from areas devastated by HIV. The number of African immigrants diagnosed with HIV has been escalating rapidly, and overtook diagnoses amongst gay men for the first time in 2001. One quarter of all those being treated for HIV in Britain are African immigrants.

Multi-culturalism does enrich Britain's culture, but there is obviously a diminishing scale of returns. A population of 30 per cent of ethnic minorities will not obviously enrich the culture that much more than a population of 15 per cent.

This can be seen most clearly in the restaurant industry, where saturation has to be reached at some point. I would guess (though I may be wrong) that most or certainly many parts of Britain have reached saturation with Indian restaurants.

The celebraters of multi-culturalism often point to surveys that show that white natives say they like living in multi-cultural Britain. However since saying you don't like living in multi-cultural Britain is tantamount to declaring yourself a racist, the findings may not totally represent the way people feel.

In contrast, a BBC poll in May 2002 showed that 47 per cent of whites said they felt immigration had harmed society in the last 50 years, compared with 28 per cent who felt it had benefited Britain. Of course, this may well be racism, but it is extraordinarily patronising to say that something is good for someone when they say that it isn't. Likewise, I have never heard of people in the mono-racial parts of Britain ask for Asians and blacks to move to their communities to save them from their mono-cultural *ennui*.

Indeed, there is evidence that white people are not drawn to, but repelled from, communities with large ethnic minorities. The fact that boroughs like Newham and Brent now have white minorities, and towns like Leicester are expected to have white minorities in ten years time, suggests a degree of white flight (a well documented phenomenon in the US). There is evidence of white flight from certain schools, with white parents trying to make sure that their children do not go to schools where they would be in a small minority (being in a minority is not easy for anyone). In central London schools, black and Asian pupils now outnumber white ones. A poll by the BBC showed that three quarters of white people said they thought other white people moved away from areas of large ethnic minorities. These are not signs of a country at ease with itself, and obviously wouldn't happen in a mono-racial one.

The multi-cultural lobby is increasingly saying that people in Britain must 'celebrate diversity' and that 'diversity is strength'. There probably are many strengths in diversity, having a mixture of skills, abilities, and personalities in a society ensures that you have scientists, lorry drivers and writers. But it really is the triumph of hope over experience to insist that cultural diversity in a wider sense is an undiluted strength. Indeed, all too many countries have been destroyed by their diversity. Try and tell the people of Northern Ireland that the mono-religion of the Republic to the South is a weakness, and their diversity of having Catholics and Protestants is a strength. Try and tell the Hutus and Tutsis of Rwanda that diversity is strength, or the Muslims and Hindus who are massacring each other in Gujarat, or the Jews and Palestinians in Israel, or the perpetually warring ethnic groups in Afghanistan, or the inhabitants in former Yugoslavia, which has ripped itself apart in a succession of ethnic-based conflicts.

It is all too clear that while diversity may be strength in some abstract sense, it can also be the recipe for utter devastation and ruinous conflict. It is the fear of that, presumably, which drives the multi-cultural lobby to protest so loudly that diversity is strength. If it really were a strength they wouldn't have to shout about it so loudly.

As I write this, the UK is heading for war with Iraq, and even moderate Muslim leaders are warning the government of the impact on social relations with Britain's two million strong Muslim community if Britain does attack another Muslim country (the less moderate leaders are warning that it will bring suicide bombing to Britain). Whatever the merits or demerits of war on Iraq, it is hardly a national strength to have a large minority with such divided loyalties during war.

Celebrating the benefits of a multi-cultural society should not blind us to the potential dangers of large-scale immigration without integration. The policies in the UK are ensuring large and growing parallel communities which are dividing many British towns, which are different in race, religion, language and don't interact socially or at work. Northern Ireland has been devastated by divisions between two groups who are visually and linguistically indistinguishable, and which are both Christian. Obviously, they have a divisive history that fuels the troubles, but in many towns in Britain the divisions between white and ethnic minority communities which are visually distinctive and have different religions are passing down to the third generation and acquiring history as they go.

In mainland Europe, there has been increasing concern that continued large-scale immigration without integration could lead to chaos. In June 2002 the senior European Commissioner Frits Bolkestein, a Dutch Liberal, warned in a lecture in The Hague, called 'An Uncertain Europe in a World of Upheaval', that integration of immigrants had failed and the situation was still deteriorating. He said the scenario of 'Europe in shambles' that had been set out by Dutch academics should be given 'serious reflection', and warned:

> We should restrict economic migration and boost the integration of minorities within the framework of the values which our liberal and democratic societies have produced. There should always be room for genuine political refugees. But most migrants come for economic reasons. Their presence worsens current problems of integration in urban areas and burdens social security systems. If the flow of migrants should remain uncontrolled, Europe would be importing poverty while the countries of origin would lose a productive part of their population.

27

Should all mono-racial societies be made multi-racial?

If the benefits of turning a mono-racial society into a multi-racial one—cultural enrichment and strength through diversity—are real, they should in theory apply to all mono-racial societies. However, there is curious silence from the pro-immigration lobby on the need to make the world's remaining mono-racial societies—basically, all the non-white host ones—multi-racial.

I have not heard claims that the Chinese should be forced to accept a hundred million (scaled up to their population of over one billion) Africans, Indians, Arabs and whites to boost their economy (already the fastest growing in the world). Or that Nigerians should accept millions of Arabs, Chinese, Indians and whites to make their country stronger through celebrating diversity (Muslims and Christians are already regularly killing each other in the North of the country). Or that Indians should accept a hundred million Arabs, Chinese, Africans and white people to enrich their culture (one of the richest cultures on the planet, and already absorbing influences from elsewhere). Or that Saudi Arabia should be forced to accept millions of blacks, Indians, whites and Chinese to save them from their boring mono-culture (there is not even one Christian church in Saudi Arabia).

I would expect that if such proposals were made, they would meet some rather stiff opposition from the Chinese, Nigerians, Arabs and Indians. I would then also expect the pro-immigration lobby to tell them that such opposition would have to be ignored because it is just racism.

Unless the pro-immigration lobby is prepared to say that the Chinese, Africans, Arabs and Indians should be culturally enriched, economically enhanced and socially diversified by accepting large-scale immigration from the rest of the world against the wishes of the majority of the population, then telling European countries that they should is just an exercise in double standards and hypocrisy. All people have a right to decide what sort of society they want to live in, and a right to have their concerns listened to, whatever the colour of their skin.

How large-scale immigration without integration fragments society

Imagine if you wanted to design the perfect immigration policy guaranteed to fragment society and lead to conflicts of interest between immigrants and natives. It should have these four main ingredients:

- it should be large-scale and rapid, so communities of immigrants can grow quickly without having to integrate or learn much about the country they have moved to. Rapid large-scale immigration will also ensure that public infrastructure, public services and the native population don't have time to adapt, helping to ensure congestion, shortages and lack of understanding.
- it should be self-selecting, so that the most recent immigrants chose the ones that follow behind them. This will ensure that immigrants don't have to make new friends or find a spouse in their new country, but can simply bring them from their old country. This helps ensure that immigrants have no incentive to integrate, and can instead live in close-knit communities that have little interaction or identification with the host population or other immigrant communities.
- no attempt should be made to encourage integration, but each community should be encouraged to see itself as different from the host population. Immigrants should not need to speak the mother tongue, all public services should be provided in their native language, they should be provided with schools that cater specifically for immigrant communities to ensure their children never get to know native children. While all immigrant culture should be celebrated, the host culture should be ritually denigrated, so that immigrant communities don't want to feel part of it, and don't want to identify with it. The host

community should have as little self-identity as possible to ensure that it is almost impossible for immigrants to adopt that identity. Immigrants should be from as different a culture as possible to the host community, to minimise any chance that a mutual understanding and respect might build up. Ideally, they should be allowed to bring religious leaders over from their home country who know nothing about the host country, but feel that is no hindrance to denouncing it and telling the immigrants why they don't want to be part of it.

- They should be a different race from the host community, to ensure that they are visibly different, and that all their descendants will remain visibly different, to make assimilation more difficult for their children and grand-children.

This, of course, is almost a perfect description of much of Britain's immigration policy, and much of that of the rest of Europe before the rise of the far Right in 2002. The level of immigration to Britain is at historically unprecedented levels, being the equivalent of a city the size of Cambridge every six months. Most of the immigration is through family reunion, or people who have friends and family who help them in. The prevailing belief in multi-culturalism and lack of self-assertion as to what it means to be British or English (compared to American or Canadian say), almost guarantees that immigrants will be alienated from the host community. Ugandan Asians integrated reasonably well because it was a one-off exodus, and their community wasn't continually refreshed by bringing friends and family over. Jews before the Second World War obviously integrated perfectly—indeed it is probably fair to say that many of the immigrants believe that their children have integrated too well and lost their cultural identity. Immigrants from Australasia and North America integrate very well because they are from the same culture, speak the same language, and aren't prone to large chain-migration effects.

Immigrants from Europe, East and West, integrate well, certainly after one generation, because their children just meld into the general population. A large number of Italians and Poles arrived in London after the Second World War, but their children are as culturally British as those whose have been here for countless generations.

Immigrants from India, Africa and the West Indies have integrated with varying degrees of success—many have integrated very well, others less so. The growing sub-culture of alienated black young men is a worrying sign of social fragmentation that is causing a great amount of stress in many communities.

However, there has been less integration among Pakistani and Bangladeshi communities in Northern towns. After two or three generations, there is little sign of integration improving, but more of increasing social fragmentation, as official reports into Bradford attest. Bradford Council published a report saying that the Bangladeshis and Pakistanis are 'colonising' the town, and want Muslim-only areas and Sharia law.

29

How current immigration patterns fuel racial tensions

The current scale and pattern of immigration is likely to steadily increase racial tensions in Britain. Because it is not accepted by the majority of British people and is on a scale that is clearly affecting their lives, the white majority may well increasingly resent immigrants. The resentment may also end up being targeted at British visible ethnic minorities whom British people may not distinguish from immigrants.

A large component of immigration is simply the result of lack of enforcement of immigration regulations, with probably around a million immigrants either clandestine or with no legal permission to stay but having avoided deportation.

There is a danger that, as a result, all immigrants will increasingly be seen by British people as illegitimate. It can be difficult to distinguish between illegal and legal immigrants, and the scale of unauthorised immigration merely raises the suspicion in the minds of many British people that everyone who even vaguely fits their stereotype of an illegal immigrant is one. This severely damages the trust there needs to be between British people and immigrants. The scale of unauthorised immigration into the UK is also in danger of creating an underclass of people who cannot legally join mainstream society, and the growth of such an underclass will also worsen racial tensions, as it has in many European countries such as France and Spain.

The record scale of immigration makes integration more difficult—it is difficult to integrate the population of a city the size of Cambridge that is moving to Britain from the Third World every six months. The Ugandan Asians integrated well, but the scale of immigration is now such that we are having the equivalent of the entire Ugandan

Asian immigration happening to Britain every six weeks. This stretches the official capacity to provide services that aid integration, and, by providing continuous additions to immigrant communities, means they have less incentive to integrate with the wider community. The East African Asians were sufficiently few in number that they had to go out and integrate; it is less likely that there would have been so much integration if their numbers had been perpetually swelled by continuous high-level immigration.

Instead, it would have been more likely to create separate parallel communities that live apart, work apart and socialise apart from mainstream society which they don't identify with. These parallel communities are clearly rapidly growing in many other immigrant groups—not just Bangladeshis and Pakistanis, but increasingly Turks in North London. The creation and growth of such parallel communities are also clearly damaging for race relations in Britain.

In some cases, the parallel communities end up supplanting existing British communities. In many Northern towns, and parts of London, there is white flight, with white British people moving out of neighbourhoods that have become dominated by immigrant communities. White flight is partly driven by racism, but also by the understandable desire to be surrounded by a community that you can relate to and identify with. Many British people have come to feel such foreigners in the neighbourhoods they were born and grew up in that they feel they have no option but to move, and the more this happens the more it is bound to fuel resentment of immigrants.

The scale of immigration is also such that it is clearly stretching public services. In many parts of the country, hospitals, schools and housing departments spend a large part of their resources catering for immigrant communities which suffer poor health, language difficulties and housing problems. Many doctors complain that they cannot offer their British patients the service they deserve because their services are so stretched catering for the immigrant population. Many British parents move their children out of schools because the classes are dominated by children who have limited English, making it difficult for already stretched teachers to provide the best level of education to British children. The more public services are demonstrably stretched by the record scale of immigration, and the more the native population perceive they are losing out as a result, the more they are likely to resent immigrants.

Finally, since no government has ever been elected on a platform to promote large-scale immigration, and the electorate have never been given the chance to vote on immigration in a referendum, the whole issue of immigration has a huge democratic legitimacy problem. There seems to be a widespread feeling among white Britons—particularly the more racist ones—that 'we never asked them here', and that all immigrants and all ethnic minorities are 'uninvited guests' who have no right to be here because the British people have never had a say in whether they can come or not. This is severely damaging for race relations. The democratic illegitimacy of the immigration flows to Britain is a huge block to the acceptance and welcoming of those immigrants who do come.

Race relations in Britain would be greatly improved if we had low levels of immigration that do not stretch public services, that do not lead to the creation of parallel communities, that allow for integration, and if the immigrants were coming to Britain within an immigration system that was widely accepted by the public who had confidence that it was being enforced and that all immigrants had demonstrated their right to be here. There will always be a problem with immigrants being accepted by the British public so long as the immigration system itself isn't accepted.

Confusing being pro-immigrant with being pro-immigration could also undermine efforts to improve race relations. The majority of white Briton's who want to help make ethnic minorities welcome and to flourish are likely to be unnerved if those efforts are used to promote mass immigration to the UK. It is a valid comparison to welcoming an uninvited guest to a party—you may be more than happy to do that unless it is used as an excuse to bring in dozens more uninvited guests.

When well-intentioned groups like the Commission for Racial Equality, the Joint Council for the Welfare of Immigrants and the Immigration Advisory Service step over the line from improving race relations or the lot of immigrants to promoting mass immigration to Britain, they run the danger of significantly undermining support for their very valid core objectives.

30

Why large-scale immigration is anti-democratic

Repeated surveys have shown that the majority of British people do not want large-scale immigration, and do not think that it has benefited Britain. Two recent impeccable polls include:

- 64 per cent of UK citizens, including 46 per cent of ethnic minorities, think there is too much immigration to the UK, according to a Commission for Racial Equality poll
- A poll for the BBC in 2002 found that 47 per cent of white people, and 22 per cent of blacks and Asians, thought that immigration had damaged British society over the last 50 years. In contrast, only 28 per cent of white people thought it had benefited British society, compared to 43 per cent of blacks and 50 per cent of Asians.

For those who believe in democracy, the fact that British people are opposed to large-scale immigration should be a good reason to promote immigration reform. But the pro-immigration lobby—having done its best to avoid any rational debate on immigration and to make sure the facts about it don't come out by accusing any critics of racism—clearly does not believe that the British people should have any say in the matter. This anti-democratic tendency reached its height when the Commission for Racial Equality tried to get the leaders of all parties not to talk about immigration in the run-up to the 2001 general election.

Given that British people show such strong opposition to immigration, an issue of absolutely fundamental social, economic and environmental importance, it is difficult to see any reason why their views should be so persistently and repeatedly ignored and sidelined. Unless, that is, like the fascists they routinely condemn, the pro-immigration lobby simply doesn't believe in democracy when it isn't convenient for them.

31

Why the Left is betraying its core constituency by supporting immigration

The politics of immigration are both complex and in many ways counter-intuitive. The winners from large-scale immigration are big business who get cheap labour, house-builders who get to build more houses, home-owners who see property prices rise and professionals who don't compete with immigrants but employ their services, all of which are causes of the political Right. The losers are generally the unskilled and semi-skilled, disproportionately ethnic minorities, who compete with immigrants, the environment, and people who rent their homes, all of which are causes of the Left.

And yet, because of the need to combat racism and support vulnerable immigrants, the Left is the biggest champion of immigration and the Right, generally, the most concerned. You get the bizarre spectacle of the free-market Right, who generally support free movement of goods and capital, opposing movement of people, and the Left, which tends to be sceptical about the free movement of goods and capital, using free-market arguments to support the free movement of people.

The reasons the Left support immigration so enthusiastically are both valid and invalid. Immigration is, everyone agrees, good for the immigrants, and that is a definite and indisputable benefit. The Left also enthusiastically embraces the pro-immigration cause because it probably, quite rightly, sees that much opposition to it is fuelled by racist sentiments. Therefore, in order to bash down racism, the Left puts forward as many pro-immigration arguments as possible, even if that means ignoring—or wilfully refusing to consider—all the negative impacts of immigration on other areas the Left is usually concerned about.

It is a pattern in the US, Britain and elsewhere in Europe, that once ethnic minorities reach a certain critical mass in a country, then the politics of race defines the politics of every other issue: the imperative to combat racism overwhelms any other consideration, whether it is the environment, the working class, law and order, or even disease control. That is why a Labour government can announce a massive increase in immigration and a major housebuilding programme covering the South East of England in the same week and refuse to admit there is a link between the two; it is why a Labour Department of Health can refuse to make any comment on the fact that the HIV epidemic in Britain has reached record levels because it is for the first time being driven by large-scale immigration from the part of the world most devastated by HIV—Africa. It is the reason that a Labour government can actively promote large-scale immigration, while ignoring the concerns of the white working classes in Northern towns who are more at the front end of the effects of immigration than anyone else, in terms of competing for scarce jobs and public resources, and living in increasingly fragmented and divided communities.

Until the issue of race reached prime importance, concern about immigration had been a preserve of the Left. All the original black rights campaigners in America were immigration restrictionists, because successive waves of immigrants undermined African-Americans; all the main founders of environment movements in the US were immigration restrictionists because of the impact immigration had on population growth and the natural environment; the union movement in the US has always (until a couple of years ago) been anti-immigration because it tried to protect its members' interests. Even the arguments about immigration promoting development in the Third World hardly stack up.

These are all left-wing causes, all now being betrayed by the imperative to promote immigration. There are now only vestiges of the old groups that are immigration restrictionists. Sierrans for a Sustainable US Population and the

Optimum Population Trust are anti-immigration environment groups in the US and UK, Diversity Alliance is an anti-immigration ethnic minority group, the American Engineering Association, American Workers First and the UK's Professional Contractors Association are all immigration restrictionists.

Because Britain only has a short history of large-scale immigration, the historic politics are less well defined, but the end point is almost identical to the US. The Right have been silenced on the issue, and the Left is betraying the interests of many of its key constituents—existing ethnic minorities, the environment, the working class—in the headlong rush to embrace the cause of immigration. Having abandoned its core constituents, the Left should not be surprised if its core constituents—such as the working classes in Northern cities—then abandon the Left.

32

Why the pro-immigration lobby are responsible for promoting fascism in Europe

The pro-immigration lobby, which insists on policies that utterly and irrevocably alter Western society, while effectively suppressing any legitimate debate on the issue, has successfully created in Europe the perfect conditions for a rise in fascism. Revolutions occur when people feel their way of life is threatened, and there is no democratic means for them to address their concerns. This being the twenty-first century in Europe, the revolutions are political rather than violent, but revolutions nonetheless.

By repeatedly scattering accusations of racism and trying to shame or deny a voice to any individual or group that tries to debate immigration, the pro-immigration lobby has successfully engineered a situation where all anti-immigration arguments are silenced and no mainstream party can reflect the clear public opinion.

This avoidance of honest debate legitimises those on the racist Right who claim there is a conspiracy of silence, and puts them in the politically convenient position of being the only ones that address people's concerns. The pro-immigration lobby has ensured that people with legitimate concerns about the impact of immigration—which is the majority of the people of Europe—have no choice but to vote for extremist parties.

The revolutions have swept Europe in 2002, including the instantaneous and shattering rise of Pim Fortuyn's party in the Netherlands, the destruction of the Left in France, and the incorporation of far-Right parties in the government in Denmark and Austria. The people of France didn't want to vote fascist, but one in five voted for Le Penn in a desperate attempt to get politicians to start doing their job properly.

In Britain, with its turgid political system, hatred of embarrassment, and unusually aggressive press, such a revolution has barely happened, but the conditions are such as to almost guarantee it will happen eventually. The Labour government, while trying to appear tough on asylum seekers, has far more quietly promoted its policy of mass immigration, ensuring it reaches record levels. At the same time, the opposition Conservative party—which has traditionally been the partly of immigration restriction —has become so paranoid about accusations of racism that it has refused to comment on any issues relating to immigration.

The result is that those in Britain concerned about the demographic, economic and cultural impact of the unprecedented wave of immigration have no choice but to give their support to the racist British National Party. The party only won three council seats in local elections in 2002, but that was triple its previous level of support, and included a win in a middle-class area. As immigration rises, and frustration with immigration rises, it is likely more and more people will overcome the shame of voting for the BNP, hold their nose and put a tick in their box.

Those of us concerned about racism, racial violence, and the shattering of a fragmented society, can only look on this with trepidation. But the fault lies with the anti-democratic pro-immigration lobby. The only way to stop it is to allow a legitimate debate—not just on asylum—but on the levels of immigration of all sorts that are transforming British society and the British way of life in ways that the large majority of British people don't like, and to have an immigration policy that commands public acceptance rather than generates public anger.

33

Why Europe doesn't have a moral duty to accept immigration

When the economic and demographic arguments for large-scale immigration crumble, pro-immigrationists frequently fall back on moral arguments, saying that Europe has a moral duty to accept immigration, giving a variety of usually historical reasons. One is that having colonised much of the developing world, Europe is responsible for destabilising it and hindering its development, and so must accept responsibility for the consequences in terms of economic migration and asylum seekers. Another argument is that Europe has startling wealth in a world dominated by poverty and we have no right to insist on keeping all this wealth to ourselves. It is often said that Europe got its wealth by plundering the developing world, and so has a moral duty to give it back.

These arguments are often quickly espoused by the immigrants from the developing world themselves. A BBC-online debate contained the following contribution:

> A strong thirst for wealth once took the British all over the world. Ironically now it's payback time. *Khairul Hasan, UK*

In a forum run by Bradford City Council to promote understanding between the white and Asian communities, one [presumably Asian] correspondent wrote:

> All I hear is moan, moan, moan. Well I tell u what get my goat u English were not complaining when u wonderfully took over the Indian subcontinent, got what u needed (Example: the crown jewels I think the crown steals is more appropriate). And White flight? I think u are more than accustomed to it u have been doing that for centuries in and around the world once u had pillaged, gorged and sent back what u needed. Guess what? What goes around comes around.

Email responses to articles of mine have repeatedly continued this theme. One correspondent wrote:

> It is indicative of the 'chickens coming home to roost' phenomenon, spread out over decades. You screw over enough parts of the world, they're [*sic*] children will eventually settle in your own backyard. After all, Britain MUST be the best place on earth, considering that your ancestors beat that notion into mine, right?

A Ghanaian immigrant to the UK wrote:

> It is only the naïve who believed they could celebrate the achievements of Empire and not pay for some its consequences. My response to Mr Browne's call for the people of Britain to decide who settles and who doesn't is this: If it is all right for people of British origin to displace natives of the countries mentioned above [US, Canada, Australia]; if it is all right for the Colonial Office to mobilise people in these countries to fight for Empire in Burma, India and the South Pacific, then surely it is all right for their descendants to enjoy the fruits of those struggles and sacrifices.

This argument was repeated to me by one of Britain's most celebrated race commentators, who said to me: 'It's a case of the Empire strikes back'.

An interesting element of these arguments is that they drop the pretence that large-scale Third World immigration to the West is somehow in the West's interest: phrases such as 'paying for the consequences', 'empire strikes back', 'chickens coming home to roost', 'what goes around comes around' and 'payback time' are the language of revenge. Europe, and particularly the UK, must pay for its past misdeeds. This is immigration as historical retribution.

I certainly agree that Europe—and the developed world in general—must accept moral responsibility for helping those that are less fortunate, but that is a very weak argument for immigration. Immigration is a very ineffective development policy and only helps a tiny proportion of people in the Third World (see chapter 34).

Unless you believe that the sins of the grandparents should be visited on the grandchildren (a biblical concept of justice that is a contravention of the European Convention of Human Rights), then the concept of 'payback' only holds if you believe that those in Europe are richer than they would other wise be because of imperialism, and that those in the developing world are poorer than they would have been without imperialism. In other words, some element of redistribution is morally justifiable if present generations are gaining unfair advantage as a result of the sins of previous generations. This is certainly the case in the white settler colonies of the USA, Canada, Australia and New Zealand, where the mainstream society that has benefited so much from the land has a huge moral duty to help disadvantaged indigenous people.

However, the historical argument that it is payback time for Europe destabilising the rest of the world can at best only apply to a few European countries, principally the UK, Portugal and France. Norway, Finland, Denmark, Sweden, Switzerland, Austria, Greece and Ireland have never in modern times had empires in the Third World; Italy effectively only had Abyssinia for a short while before being beaten by the Abyssinians in battle. Germany had a small empire in Southern Africa for a short while until it was divested of it all after defeat in the First World War nearly a century ago.

Some European countries did have empires but they are not significant sources of immigration. Spain had a large empire in South America (as well as the Philippines and western Sahara) but it was a very long time ago, and there is limited migration from there. Portugal controlled Brazil before it claimed independence, and relatively few Brazilians want to move permanently to their former colonial owner, although those from its former African colonies do.

It is possible to argue that Britain is responsible for the conditions that create the desire to migrate from India, Pakistan, Bangladesh, much of sub-Saharan Africa and the Middle East with varying degrees of conviction, depending on the area (although Britain also helped create the developed nations of the US, Canada, Australia and New Zealand, which are all large recipients of Third World immigration). Likewise with France and North Africa.

But most of that is a long time ago, and historical justifications—also often used for genocides and wars—have to have a cut-off point at some time. It is also very patronising to Indian governments over the last 50 years to say that they are not responsible for the state of the country (its problems and very many successes) at the start of the twenty-first century. Much of the British empire in Africa was held for a relatively short period and yet the immigration argument would mean a permanent penance for a time-limited sin. Almost all academics on the subject agree that the present state of Africa is the result of its appalling post-independence rulers, not the result of the actions of the West.

There is also a widespread but economically fallacious view that Europe's present wealth is somehow the result of plundering the developing world a hundred years ago. Colonies certainly were a major source of wealth to the imperial powers such as Britain at the turn of the twentieth century. But the British economy has virtually nothing in common now with what it was 100 or even 50 years ago. Wealth has grown immeasurably since then and the industries that existed then—textiles, ship-building etc—have now disappeared.

Looking around the developed world, it is actually often the case that those that aren't burdened by the history of an empire are the richest. Ireland has overtaken the UK in GDP per capita, but never had an empire. Scandinavia, Switzerland and Luxembourg are some of the richest regions of Europe and never had an empire. You have to divorce yourself from reality to argue that Germany's economic success is somehow to do with the fact that it controlled South West Africa before the First World War. If large empires made countries rich, Portugal would be one of the richest countries in Europe, but it is one of the poorest. The US, Canada, Australia and New Zealand are all rich countries that never had empires. All mainstream economists agree that Britain's wealth at the start of the twenty-first century is all to do with sustained improvements in productivity, and nothing to do with its historical empire.

34

Why immigration to rich countries harms poor countries

The best and most unanswerable argument for immigration is that it is good for immigrants; otherwise they wouldn't immigrate, or having immigrated would return. This is what ultimately drives all the immigration pressure from the developing world onto the West: millions of individual decisions to improve their lives.

But this does not mean that it is particularly good for those they leave behind. Indeed, recruiting the most energetic, entrepreneurial or educated from the developing world is not just a very inefficient development policy, it is positively damaging to many countries, particularly those in Africa.

It sustains poverty in the developing world by removing politically stabilising middle classes, removing the wealth-creating and tax-paying professional and entrepreneurial classes, and it sustains dictatorial régimes by removing awkward dissidents.

Immigration can help global development if people move from poor countries, learn skills, and return to their home country enriching it with their skills. But people who learn skills successfully in the West rarely return (as evidenced by the fact that immigration from the Indian subcontinent to the UK is 12 times the rate it is from the UK to India). Studies in the US suggest only 25 per cent of immigrants from developing nations return.

Immigration can help relieve poverty in the Third World because people who work in the West supply remittances to their families back home, which is a very well-targeted form of aid thought to total around $60bn a year. But for that to be sustained, it requires perpetual migration from poor to rich countries, which is not only unsustainable because of the effects on the rich countries, but also puts poor countries in a perpetual economic dependency on rich countries. It also encourages poor countries to develop remittance economies based on the sustained export of their best people, rather than address the root causes of their poverty and help ensure that their country is a place where people want to live rather than leave. When emigration becomes a corner stone of the economic policy, there is no incentive for governments to do things that ensure that people want to stay.

The more that western countries target their immigration policies to highly skilled people, the worst the imbalance will be. There is little chance of development if every go-getter moves from the developing world to America or Europe. As immigration to the West accelerates, the brain drain is becoming increasingly frustrating to many nations. Sixteen different countries—including many of those devastated by AIDS in Southern Africa—have pleaded with Britain to stop recruiting their nurses, whom they paid to train out of scarce public resources, and whom they need far more than the UK does.

One of the things that Africa needs is educated people, but a study by Britain's Department for International Development found that three-quarters of Africa's emigrants have university education, and roughly half of Asia's and South America's. According to Lindsay Lowell of the Pew Hispanic Centre, 12 per cent of Mexico's population with higher education live in the US, and 75 per cent of Jamaica's. Jamaican newspapers repeatedly report that their education system is collapsing because most of its teachers just move to the West. About 30 per cent of highly educated Ghanaians and Sierra Leoneons live abroad. The *Economist* magazine, which is usually staunchly pro-immigration, recently surveyed the issue and concluded on its cover: 'How emigration hurts poor countries'.

Ghana, one of the most stable and free African countries, suffers particularly badly because the high quality of its free education system makes it easy for its graduates to emigrate. Earlier graduates make emigration easier for later graduates through the usual networks, and plant the idea of emigration as the high point of education. The end result is that a valuable education system which is essential to development is undermined because it is turned into a stepping stone for emigration of Ghana's most talented. The *Accra Mail* thundered against the devastating effects of this brain drain to the West in an editorial in 12 August 2002, which is so eloquent it is worth quoting at length:

> The unfortunate and demoralizing fact in this saga is that, even though the Republic of Ghana continues to invest stupendous amounts of money she can barely afford in the education of its youth, she most tragically does not have much to show for all its aggrandisement, since she has failed to retain the highly skilled workforce (*la crème de la crème*). It seems that our country is 'eaten' by the Western world. 'All those who have money, all those who have accomplished something, who bought a house or had one built, it is because they have money,' from Europe or America. Is this why we are so chained? Once that green evil gets under our skin, we are a goner, nothing else makes any sense anymore except to leave this hell-hole Ghana. No more poverty—all one sees are cities of light and joy; a land where the magical green paper is 'easily' made, where the streets are 'paved' with gold. People have only two things on their mind, Europe and America. After graduation, what preoccupies most graduates is how to leave a land they have come to associate with wretchedness, misery, and abject poverty as compared to those honey-laced 'civilised' places where, we have come to believe 'everything is possible'. When the country needs most of these graduates to put their skills at its disposal, what we witness is one in every four of these young people studiously, feverishly, and most pathetically filling visa application forms at a consulate of a North American or a Western European country to forestall the sudden doom they foretell for themselves. No matter that these embassies humiliate them daily; no matter that there are many failed attempts; the queue for visas gets longer by the minute. The desperate knows no shame.
>
> The end result is an impressive number of doctors, dentists, opticians, lab technicians, nurses and others in almost every specialized field in health care who graduate every year from our institutions gratis, compliments of the Republic of Ghana. Next they simply hang around to count the number of days when the opportunity will present itself for them to hop on to the next available transcontinental flight to somewhere in Europe or America where they will provide their services to those communities which never spent a dime on their education or training.

In 2002, economists at Addis Ababa university did a study claiming that the loss of 20,000 professionals a year from Africa to the West costs Africa about $4bn a year: they claimed, for example, that there are dozens of Ethiopian professors of economics in the USA, but only one in Ethiopia. The economists claimed that the brain drain was so serious and hindering development to such an extent that the West should pay compensation to Africa. The study was presented to the Organisation of Social Science Research in East Africa by its author, Dr Dejene Aredo, who said:

> It is a problem, because there is a huge deficit of manpower in developing countries. Highly qualified professionals are migrating to the West when we don't have enough of them here.

As well as the brain drain, immigration leads to a 'dissident drain'. Those dissatisfied with a country and able enough to escape it to the West are precisely the ones who would lead to reform from within, helping improve the conditions within the country. Communist totalitarianism in Eastern Europe collapsed because of the actions of internal dissidents—indeed post-communist Eastern Europe was largely led by former dissidents such as Lech Walensa of Poland, and Vaclav Havel of Czechoslovakia. In contrast, Cuba remains a communist state largely because almost all its dissidents are not living in Cuba but in the US. Indeed this is precisely the reason that the dictator Fidel Castro is happy to let dissidents leave Cuba—he would much prefer they spent their time trying to improve their lives in the US, rather than trying to improve the political situation in Cuba.

The imbalances in the world are so extreme in terms of numbers that immigration can only, in any politically or economically feasible future, play a tiny part in the development of the Third World. Simple numbers dictate that few of the 1.1 billion people who live in India or 1.3bn who live in China will ever live in the West. The immigration of 35,000 Indians a year to Britain is quite significant for Britain, which has a population of roughly one twentieth of that of India, but it is insignificant for India.

Roy Beck, the painstakingly liberal leader of the US immigration restrictionist group NumbersUSA, wrote in 1996:

> There's nothing we could ever do—we could take three million, five million a year; we could completely destroy the environmental resources of this country; we could completely destroy the job markets; we could destroy the social fabric of this nation—there's no way that we could ever relieve the pressure [on people in the sending countries] by immigration. The only hope for most of the impoverished people in the world is to be helped where they live, to bloom where they are planted.

Much of the immigration pressure on the West is because of the demographic pressure in the developing world—suffering the consequences of large and growing populations. But using the West as a demographic safety valve, an overflow for excessive numbers of people in the developing world, will merely encourage the overpopulation of the world as a whole.

There is significant evidence that high levels of emigration from the Third World actively encourage high levels of fertility. The title of the 1991 study by Ann Brittain in the journal *Social Biology* speaks for itself: 'Anticipated Child Loss to Migration and Sustained High Fertility in an East Caribbean Population'. It found that high levels of emigration from areas in the Caribbean were correlated with sustained high birth rates, whereas in areas of low emigration birth rates fell as the population grew. It concluded that if mothers expected certain numbers of their children to emigrate, they would have more children.

A 1990 study 'Migration and the Demographic Transition: A West Indian Example', from the Institute of Social and Economic Research, University of the West Indies, Kingston, Jamaica, looked at birth, death and emigration rates from 1880 to 1967 for the island of St Barthelemy. It found that increases in emigration were followed five years later by increases in the birth rate.

As a result, using the West as a demographic safety valve for over-population in the Third World merely enhances the ultimate over-population of the world as a whole. Professor

Virginia Abernethy Vanderbilt University in her 1994 paper *U.S. Immigration Fuels World-Wide Population Growth*, wrote:

> The prospect of being able to immigrate to the United States —legally or illegally—may actually increase suffering because it allows high-fertility countries to put off taking action on overpopulation. If our impulses that seem in the short run to do good lead ultimately to worldwide disaster and most quickly to disaster in the countries we wish to help, they are not humanitarian. Not tightening our borders is destructive because it blocks environmental feedback that should be a warning sign of limits.

It is difficult to reach any conclusion other than that if your ultimate aim is for developing nations to become stable, sustainable, and enjoying a quality of life and self-respect high enough that people want to live in them rather than leave them, then, in the long run, immigration hinders that rather then helps it. If your sole aim is to help the Third World as a whole develop, you would not choose encouraging emigration to the West as the answer.

35

Why the Third World immigration pressure a wake-up call to rich countries to do more to help poor ones

The current immigration pressure facing the entire Western world is a reflection of the fact that the West is rich, while much of the world is poor; television and mass media have taught the poor about how the rich live; and cheap global transport has made it possible for unprecedented numbers of people to seek that life. For the first time in history, the poor have the means, the motive and the knowledge to come to the rich world.

At the same time there seems to be widespread compassion fatigue in the West, having discovered there is a lot of poverty in the world, and that it is hard to do anything about it. Coverage of foreign news is falling, and aid budgets are shrinking.

But no longer is it possible just to shut it out, or only watch it on TV programmes with dwindling audiences or on soul-searching round-the-world trips. For the first time, the poverty and deprivation of the developing world is being visited on the door steps of the rich world.

This immigration pressure is not something we can or should ignore. The rich world has a right to keep it at bay in order to preserve its own way of life, but it also has a duty to tackle the causes.

This immigration pressure is a wake-up call to the West to take the plight of the developing world seriously, as a primary focus of government policies across the board. Aid should be augmented, but targeted more at people and their support groups rather than governments, and aimed at improving productivity in the Third World rather than just humanitarian ends. Aid must be untied from trade and other contracts that merely help to serve the developed world. In trade policy, the West must not try to shut out cheap producers in the Third World, and must scrap all tariffs against the poor who wish to sell to the rich. In agricultural policy, the West must scrap subsidies for agriculture that prop up economically unviable industries, and have the effect of keeping out farmers from the developing world. The rich world must stop dumping cheap goods it can't sell at home in the developing world, if it harms local producers. It must encourage the exchange of knowledge and information.

The fact that African immigration has overtaken gay sex as the main cause of HIV in Britain is a sign that the Europe can no longer ignore the entirely preventable AIDS holocaust consuming the continent next door. But the solution is to treat the majority where they live, rather than the small number who can make it to Britain to access HIV treatment on the NHS.

No longer can the West just pay lip service to redressing the unbalances in the world. Helping balance out the world is no longer just in the interests of the poor, but in the self-interest of the rich.

36

Future perfect: a world without barriers, but not while it is so unbalanced

I share the dream of many in the pro-immigration movement of a world without barriers, finally freeing all humanity to travel and move where they wish, to make the most out of their lives. This is the historic step we have taken in the European Union, freeing nearly 400 million people to live and work where they wish within 15 countries. This policy has been an immense success—migration has been modest, balanced and almost totally beneficial—and this is not the subject of any political controversy. It puts the Americans and Canadians—who share such similar culture, incomes and language—to shame.

It is also the situation that used to exist in the world 100 years ago, when there were no passports and no such thing as passport control. People were largely free to travel and live where they wished.

But we cannot easily go back to that era. Television, films, newspapers and the internet had vastly increased knowledge of other places in the world at the same time as global travel has become extraordinarily quick and cheap.

With travel so easy, and global wealth so imbalanced, there is now for the first time in history both the means and the motive for mass migration on a scale that the world has never seen before. One US study suggested that 400 million people in the world want to move to the US. Such flows would seriously destabilise not just the destination countries—where the changes would be permanent—but also the countries of origin, where the effects would probably wear off after a generation or so.

Travel is likely to remain as easy as it is now, but while such global imbalances in wealth exist there will be more people wanting to emigrate to Britain and Europe than we can conceivably accommodate. While more people want to move here than we can accept, we have to have immigration controls of some sort, and such controls inevitably involve denying to people something they dearly want to do.

There is no kind way out of this, except to work towards a world where such imbalances no longer exist. Only then can we once again let the barriers down.

Conclusion

Britain should decide what it wants out of immigration, and ensure the immigration system is fit for the purpose

The pattern and scale of immigration to the UK are such that it achieves very few of the aims that are claimed for it, and it has several harmful consequences in terms of rising congestion, intensified housing crisis, increasingly over-stretched public services such as schools and hospitals, rising inequalities, importing diseases such as HIV and TB, and fragmenting social cohesion. It also demonstrably fails to achieve widespread public support.

Like all policies that have profound social, economic and cultural consequences, it is important that immigration achieves public support and acceptance, otherwise there are dangers that an increasingly large proportion of the public will not only refuse to accept the pattern of immigration but also refuse to accept the immigrants themselves—they will widely be seen as illegitimate. This is harmful for the immigrants, harmful for British ethnic minorities whom the white British majority may confuse with immigrants, and so harmful to both race relations and social cohesion. There is a real danger that ethnic minorities who are born and grow up in Britain and contribute huge amounts to society will get caught in the middle between the white majority residents and the record levels of immigration that they resent.

Like most of the West, there are clearly far more people who want to live in Britain than the native inhabitants are prepared to accept, and so there have to be some controls on who is let in and why. This entails deciding roughly how many people it is desirable to let in each year, and which particular groups of people should be let in. The British people should be able to decide what the ultimate aims of immigration policy should be, and then the immigration system should aim to deliver it.

At present, the British government does not aim for a particular level of immigration, takes very little part in the decision-making process of who is legally let in and who is not, and then has very little power or ability to enforce who is let in and who is not. The immigration—through whichever route—is almost entirely self-selecting, with no actual quotas on any of categories of entry. In other words, the level and type of immigration are effectively determined by the immigrants themselves, and however many decide to come and can find a route of entry, rather than by the government or wider British public.

This is reflected in the fact that the Home Office says that it has 'no view' on the desirable level of immigration, a curious abrogation of responsibility in an important policy area. It is reflected in the fact that while Britain officially has no policy on the desirable level of immigration, it has reached the highest levels ever in British history: it is not the government deciding this, but the immigrants themselves by sheer weight of numbers. The two most common routes of entry are family reunion, which is almost always recent immigrants selecting the newer immigrants, and asylum-seekers, which is totally self-selecting.

The record net immigration to the UK is largely a passive reaction to the strong and growing immigration pressure on Britain from the Third World and Eastern Europe, and Britain's porous borders. It is not the result of a deliberate policy thought out from first principles of what the aims and scale of immigration should be, although it has been stoked up by the immigration lobby, and various government measures to give greater rights to immigrants both to stay in Britain and to bring in other immigrants, as well as some efforts to attract certain types of migrants such as nurses. Almost all the justifications of such immigration have been post-facto justifications of immigration that is already happening. Since much of this immigration is almost accidental rather than a pre-thought-out act of national policy, there are few rational justifications for it from the point of view of the wider public. As a result, many, if not most, of the post-facto justifications have relied on factual distortion or specious reasoning.

As this book has shown, Britain doesn't have a declining population; Britain doesn't have a declining workforce; it isn't faced with a demographic time bomb; immigration is no fix for an ageing society; there are no economic benefits in terms of increasing GDP per capita; Britons don't want to be culturally enriched, but, like most peoples of the world, want to preserve their culture.

Since the record net immigration is in the main a passive response to the fact that immigrants want to come to Britain and gain entry through various legal and illegal channels, the only justification is that it is in the interests of the migrants themselves. This is a perfectly valid justification in itself, but it could be used to justify as much immigration from the Third World to Britain as is necessary to ensure that there is sufficient equality of standard of living between the Third World and Britain that migrants no longer want to move to Britain.

Any rational immigration policy involves balancing the economic and humanitarian interests of the migrants with the interests of the native population, as well as the interests of the source country from whence the migrants came. At present, almost the entire balance of interest is with the migrants, taking very little account of the interests of the British citizens or the sending countries.

What are the aims and purposes of immigration?

The aim of the immigration system should simply be to combine humanitarian purposes (such as asylum and genuine husband-and-wife reunion) with maximising the economic and quality-of-life benefits of immigration to the UK population. Immigration should be able to be shown to be beneficial to the people of the UK, be sustainable, and meet with the approval of the people of the UK. Current immigration fails on all three criteria.

Immigration should not be used as a tool of demographic engineering. As countless studies have concluded, from the OECD, UN, Home Office and Council of Europe, immigration is not a 'fix' for an ageing population because immigrants grow old too. An ageing population is an inevitable consequence of people living longer and a population stabilising, and any effects of it should be mitigated by other means, such as increasing participation rates of working-age people, and transforming the pension system from a pay-as-you-go scheme to a funded scheme.

The desirable scale of net immigration—the optimal numbers of people to let in each year—comes down to an assessment of the impact on increased numbers on quality of life and the economy. For the UK, which is very densely populated, where overcrowding holds back economic growth, where the population is still naturally growing of its own accord, where the workforce is growing, where there is a housing crisis and where public services are desperately overstretched, then the ideal level of net immigration is either zero or modestly negative. If in 20 years time the UK has a falling population, and that is a considered a problem, then the optimal level of net immigration may be positive. That does not mean creating 'Fortress Britain': net immigration is the difference between the number of people who arrive each year and the number who leave. It is possible, as we have had in the past, to have zero net immigration—or balanced immigration—with large but roughly equal numbers arriving and leaving. The UK enjoys balanced migration with the rest of the developed world, with, for example, almost exactly equal numbers leaving the UK for the rest of the EU as vice versa each year.

Immigration—in terms of bringing in large-scale communities from other cultures—should not be used as a way of promoting cultural enrichment. The large majority of British people do not want to be culturally enriched, and many feel that the scale of immigration is such that enrichment is turning into submergence.

Immigration should not be used as a form of global development policy. Taking the most educated and most entrepreneurial people from the world's poorest countries is a very ineffective way to help them develop. It helps the individuals who come to the West, who are a tiny fraction of one per cent of the total in the Third World, and does nothing to ensure that help the source countries become places that people want to live in rather than leave. Development is part of immigration policy only to the extent that we have a self-interest in improving the quality of life in the Third World to reduce the migration pressure on the UK. This includes making far greater efforts to combat the entirely preventable AIDS holocaust that is devastating the continent next door.

Immigration is a net positive benefit in allowing people to go where they think their lives will be better, and improves the world economy by allowing people to go where they can get the greatest returns on their skills. Given these benefits of immigration, all countries should pursue policies of having open borders as far as this is compatible with having the level of migration flows they judge optimal for their country. This has already been done very successfully within the EU; it is not possible for the UK to do so with the developing world while such income disparities exist because it unleashes destabilising population flows. However, the UK government should pursue policies of reducing or eliminating immigration controls with countries such as Japan or South Korea where there are likely to be limited, balanced, beneficial migration flows without chain migration effects.

While roughly aiming for balance between the numbers of people arriving and leaving, Britain must decide what types of immigrants to let in. One component will obviously be UK citizens returning from living overseas, but this tends to be slightly less than the numbers leaving (because some stay overseas—there is slight net emigration). One component of arrivals should remain genuine refugees, although the number is of the order of 10,000 rather than 100,000.

Since family reunion is the biggest single category of entry (people bringing in husbands, wives, children, and parents, primarily from India, Pakistan, Bangladesh and Africa), there is no way of attaining sustainable and balanced migration without making some restrictions. This is politically sensitive, but Britain has some of the most generous family reunion provisions of any developed nation. Employers should continue to fill specific skills gaps through the work visa programme, but there should be tighter controls forcing employers to show that there is no one within the EU labour market who can do the job.

To tackle the evident abuses of the immigration system, we should also tighten up control of benefits, council housing and health services, making sure they are only available to those who are entitled to them and not to all comers, which is in effect the case at the moment. This will entail some sort of entitlement card—at the moment hospitals, schools, benefit offices and housing departments have no way of distinguishing the legitimate from the illegitimate.

Finally, once an immigration policy is decided on, it should be enforced. That means tightening up passport control, so immigration services can track overstayers, and having a tough and effective policy on deportation of illegal immigrants.

Appendix

Immigration Reform Groups around the world

There are immigration reform campaigns in many countries, motivated by a variety of reasons. I have excluded those that are explicitly racist, but included ones that are motivated by concern for quality of life, environment, social cohesion and jobs.

United Kingdom

Migration Watch UK
(www.migrationwatchuk.org)
Leading think-tank with an immigration-restrictionist stance, founded in 2001 by former British ambassador to Saudi Arabia Sir Andrew Green

The Optimum Population Trust
(www.optimumpopulation.org)
Campaigns against overpopulation in the UK for environmental and quality of life reasons, and supports zero net immigration.

Gaia Watch
(www.gaiawatch.org)
Environment group concerned about the impact of immigration on UK population and environment.

Professional Contractors Group
(www.pcgroup.org.uk)
A professional association with a variety of concerns, one of which is to ensure that employment and pay rates of British IT professionals aren't undermined by fast track visas for overseas contractors.

United States

There are literally dozens of groups in the US, many of them regional. This is just a selection of the more mainstream and more moderate ones.

Federation for American Immigration Reform
(www.fairus.org)
FAIR is a national, non-profit, grass-roots organisation lobbying for the US's immigration policies to be reformed to serve the national interest.

Center for Immigration Studies
(www.cis.org)
Leading and highly respected immigration reform think tank.

Americans for Immigration Control
(www.immigrationcontrol.com)
Founded in 1983, it claims to be the country's largest grassroots immigration lobby group with 250,000 members and supporters.

Americans for Better Immigration
(www.betterimmigration.com)
Its website declares: 'Americans for Better Immigration is a non-profit, non-partisan organization which lobbies Congress for reductions in immigration numbers. ABI believes the problem with immigration today is not the individual immigrant but the numbers. "Better" immigration is lower immigration.'

Diversity Alliance for a Sustainable America
(www.diversityalliance.org)
An ethnic minority immigration restriction group founded by a Vietnamese immigrant who used to be an immigration lawyer.

United to Secure America
(www.secureamerica.info)
A national coalition that believes that immigration should be in the national interest, and that 'to protect all Americans, we must restore integrity to America's immigration system and effectively enforce our laws'.

NumbersUSA
(www.numbersusa.com)
A liberal immigration reduction lobby group. NumbersUSA describes itself as 'a non-profit, non-partisan, public policy organization that favors an environmentally sustainable and economically just America. It opposes efforts to use federal immigration policies to force mass U.S. population growth and to depress wages of vulnerable workers. NumbersUSA.com is pro-environment, pro-worker, pro-liberty and pro-immigrant. Activists in the NumbersUSA.com network are Americans of all races'.

Project USA
(www.projectusa.org)
A pro-immigrant group that campaigns for an 'immigration time out', with advertising campaigns around the country.

The Coalition for the Future American Worker
(www.americanworker.org)
CFAW is an umbrella organization of professional trade groups, population/environment organizations, and immigration reform groups aimed at representing the interests of American workers and students in the formulation of immigration policy.

Hire American Citizens
(www.hireamericancitizens.org)
Campaigns to make sure American workers don't lose out to the work visa programme.

The American Engineering Association
(www.aea.org)
Campaigns against too many guest worker visas to protect the employment interests of US engineers.

Negative Population Growth
(www.npg.org)
Campaigns for a smaller US and world population, with a heavy emphasis on reducing immigration to the US.

Sierrans for US Population Stablization
(www.susps.org)
SUSPS is a splinter group from the US's main environment group, the Sierra Club, after it abandoned its long-held policy of restricting immigration to the US.

Carrying Capacity Network
(www.carryingcapacity.org)
Campaigns for an environmentally sustainable population.

Scientists for Population Reduction
(www.scientists4pr.org)
Run by a collection of science professors concerned about the environment.

Population Connection
(www.populationconnection.org)
Previously called Zero Population Growth, this group wants to stablise the US population, and believes 'that immigration pressures on the US population are best relieved by addressing factors which compel people to leave their homes and families and emigrate to the United States'.

Australia

Sustainable Population Australia
(www.population.org.au)
Formed in 1988 by people who felt that 'the issue of population numbers was overlooked, or regarded as too contentious, by many of those striving to preserve Australia's ecological heritage'.

Canada

Canada First Immigration Reform Committee
(www.canadafirst.net)
Its rather alarmist group website declares: 'AIDS, multi-drug-resistant TB, hepatitis, malaria, ethnic gang violence and drug pushing—poorly screened immigration and "refugees" endanger you and your family'.

Netherlands

Club Ten Million
(http://home.wxs.nl/~tienmilj/eng/)
Campaigns to slowly return the population of the Netherlands from 16 million to 10 million, with the slogan 'more humanity with fewer humans'.

Website Immigration Forums
(www.vdare.com)
An editorial collective, largely led by Peter Brimelow, a British-born immigrant to America, and author of *Alien Nation: Common Sense about America's Immigration Disaster*

http://heather.cs.ucdavis.edu/pub/Immigration/Index.html
Immigration Forum of Norman Matloff, professor of computer studies at University of California.

Bibliography

Abernethy, V. (1994) Vanderbilt University, *Immigration Fuels World-Wide Population Growth*

Borjas, G.J. (1996) 'The New Economics of Immigration', *Atlantic Monthly* Vol. 278 Issue 5 pp. 72-78

Borjas, G.J. and Freeman, R.B. (1997) 'Findings We Never Found', *New York Times* 10 December

Borjas, G.J. (1999) *Heaven's Door: Immigration Policy and the American Economy*, Princeton: Princeton University Press

Brittain, A.W. (1990) 'Migration and the Demographic Transition: A West Indian Example', *Social and Economic Studies*, Vol. 39 No. 3. Kingston, Jamaica: Institute of Social and Economic Research, University of the West Indies

Brittain, A.W. (1991) 'Anticipated Child Loss to Migration and Sustained High Fertility in an East Caribbean Population', *Social Biology* Vol. 38 No. 1-2 pp. 94-112

Camarota, S.A. (1999) *Importing Poverty: Immigration's Impact on the Size and Growth of the Poor Population in the United States,* Washington DC: Centre for Immigration Studies

CIS (1994) *Immigration and the Labor Market*, Washington DC: Centre for Immigration Studies

Collacott, M. (September 2002) *Canada's Immigration Policy: the need for major reform*, Fraser Institute, Canada

Coleman, D. (2000) 'Reproduction and Survival in an Unknown World', *People and Place*, Vol. 8, No. 2, Centre for Population and Urban Research, Monash University

Coleman, D. (November 2000) 'Migration to Europe: a critique of the new establishment consensus', speech to Workshop on Demographic Specificity and Integration of Migrants, Federal Institute of Population Research, Germany

Coleman, D. (October 2000) *Who's afraid of low support ratios? A UK response to the UN Population Division report on 'Replacement Migration'*, Paper presented to UN Expert Group meeting in New York to discuss 'Replacement Migration'

Coleman, D. (2002) 'Replacement Migration', or why everyone's going to have to live in Korea: a fable for our times from the United Nations', *Philosophical Transactions of the Royal Society* B 357

The Economist (28 September 2002) 'How Emigration Hurts Poor Countries'

Feld, S. (2000) University of Liege 'Active population growth and immigration hypotheses in Western Europe', *European Journal of Population* Volume 16

Feld, S. (August 2001) University of Liege *Labour Force Trends in the European Union (2000-2025) and International Manpower Movements*, Paper presented to General Population Conference, Salvador, Brazil

Government Actuary Department (2002) *National Population Projections, 2000 based*, Series PP2, No. 23, The Stationery Office, London

Health and Welfare Canada (1989) *Charting Canada's Future: A Report of the Demographic Review*, Ottawa: Health and Welfare Canada

Hewlett, S.A. (2002) *Baby Hunger: The New Battle for Motherhood*, Atlantic Books

Home Office (2001) *Control of Immigration: Statistics United Kingdom 2000* Cm 5315, The Stationery Office, London

Home Office (2001) *Migration: an economic and social analysis*, Research and Development Statistics Directorate Occasional Paper No 67, Home Office, London

Home Office (2001) *International migration and the United Kingdom: recent patterns and trends*, Home Office RDS Occasional paper No 75

Home Office (2002) *The Migrant Population in the UK: fiscal effects*, Home Office RDS Occasional Paper No 77

Johnson, H.P., Tafoya, S.M. (2000) 'Trends in Family and Household Poverty', *California Counts: Population Trends and Profiles* Vol. 1 No. 3 Public Policy Institute of California

Kolankiewicz, L. and Beck, R. (2001) *Forsaking Fundamentals: The Environmental Establishment Abandons US Population Stabilization*, Centre for Immigration Studies

Macdonald Commission (1985) Minister of Supply and Services, 'Royal Commission on the Economic Union and Development Prospects for Canada', *Report* Vol. 3 Ottawa: Minister of Supply and Services

Mahony, G. (former principal race relations officer) 'Race Relations in Bradford', a supplementary report to Sir Herman Ousley (2001) 'Community Pride not Prejudice: making diversity work in Bradford'

Malkin, M. (2002) *Invasion: How America Lets Terrorists, Torturers, and Other Foreign Criminals Right Through the Front Door*, Washington: Regnery Publishing Inc

Malloy, R. (1996) *'Cast Down Your Bucket Where You Are': Black Americans on Immigration*, Washington DC: Centre for Immigration Studies

McCarthy, K. and Vernez, G. (1998) *Immigration in a Changing Economy: California's Experience*, Rand

Nihon University Population Research Institute (March 2001) Conference on Population Ageing in Industrialised Countries: Challenges and Issues, report of proceedings

OECD (2001) *Trends in Immigration and Economic Consequences*, Organisation for Economic Co-operation and Development

PIU (July 2001) *Improving Labour Market Achievements for Ethnic Minorities in British Society*, Performance and Innovation Unit, Cabinet Office

Punch, A. and Pearce, D. (2001) *Europe's Population and Labour Market Beyond 2000*, Council of Europe

Shaw, C. (2001) 'United Kingdom Population Trends in the 21st Century', *Population Trends 103* London: The Stationery Office

Swan, N. *et al* (1991) *Economic and Social Impacts of Immigration* Ottawa: Economic Council of Canada

UN (October 1997) *Future Expectations for Below-Replacement Fertility*', United Nations Population Division

UN (2000) *Replacement Migration: is it a solution to declining and ageing populations?* United Nations Population Division

US Council of Economic Advisers (February 1994) Annual Report to the President

US National Academy of Sciences (1997) *The New Americans: Economic, Demographic, and Fiscal Effects of Immigration*

Wanless, D. (April 2002) *Securing Our Future Health: Taking a Long-Term View,* Her Majesty's Treasury